Paint a Little Square

Expanded Edition

Reflective Writings
by
Henry Tews

MOTIVATIONAL • SPIRITUAL • INSPIRATIONAL

Copyright © 2003 by Henry Tews, Sr.
All rights reserved.

Published by Graphix Products, Inc.
399 Wegner Drive
West Chicago, IL 60185

Printed in the U.S.A.
First Edition January 2001
Second Edition March 2003

ISBN 0-9749989-090000

Library of Congress Control Number: 2004101863

No part of this publication may be reproduced, stored in a retrieval system, or transmitted, in any form or by any means, electronic, mechanical, photocopying, recording, or otherwise, without the prior written permission of the publisher.

Designer: Barry Smith, West Chicago, IL
Page Production: Point West, Inc., Carol Stream, IL
Printing: Graphix Products, Inc., West Chicago, IL

"To meet Henry Tews is an experience! Immediately, his enthusiasm, his exuberance and his warmth quickly surround you. You are of immense importance to him and that fact alone is so supportive and encouraging. Henry believes you can, and before long, so do you!"

—*Most Reverend Joseph L. Imesch*
Bishop of Joliet Diocese

"Henry has successfully helped others battle some of life's most intractable scourges such as drug addiction. Over the years, he has encountered the bad and the beautiful. His stories fill us with hope."

—*Congressman Henry J. Hyde*
U.S. House of Representatives

"Henry and I share a great love of fishing. He is a master—patient, innovative and tenacious—all attributes of a great fisherman. Whether he is fishing for bass or people to help, he is a role model for all those who aspire to success one day at a time and to serenity in life."

—*Hon. Michael B. Getty*
Illinois Circuit Judge (Ret.)

"I am proud that Henry chose Addison as the home for Serenity House and assure him of the continued support of our community. He is a tireless champion for the many people served by this recovery program."

—Mayor Larry Hartwig
Village of Addison, Illinois

"Henry commands us to look beyond human frailty and see the goodness in all men. He expects us to be forgiving when forgiveness seems impossible. His message is comforting during the times when our world doesn't seem to make any sense at all."

—Angela Zoloto, M.S.
DuPage County Psychological Services

Dedicated to my grandchildren:
Alison, Evy, Amy, Paula, David, Jamie,
Johnathon, and Natalie Tews, and Catherine Cudahy

Thanks to my wife, Diane, for her love, support and encouragement over the forty-one years of our marriage. Her ability to critique objectively assisted in bringing focus when my writing sometimes rambled.

I thank my sons, Henry, David, Christopher and Jason Tews and my daughter, Jennifer Cudahy for their unquestioning love.

Jan Licht, a wonderful person and editor, helped me cross my i's and dot my t's.

Barbara Miles, Dennis Kaplan, and Lisa Snipes interpreted my scribbles and helped put them to print.

Thanks to Colleen Morgan whose interest in these stories and expertise as a liaison brought this project to the publisher.

Special thanks for the encouragement and support of Dr. Keith Armstrong.

Those of us who have made the prevention and treatment of substance abuse a priority in our lives understand all too well the significance of Henry Tews, his work and the founding of Serenity House.

We have been touched many times and in many ways by the stories and personal experiences of men, women and children who have battled an alcohol or drug problem, or who have been affected by another's substance abuse. By writing his experiences and memories down, Henry Tews has done us all a favor by reminding us that none of us battle alone.

Serenity House is a living testament to every person's need to comfort others and make their lives better. It is overdue that Henry Tews' stories from Serenity House should be shared with everyone in Illinois as a source of inspiration and courage.

—George H. Ryan
Governor, State of Illinois

—Lura Lynn Ryan
First Lady, State of Illinois

TABLE OF CONTENTS

Foreword	ix
To a Friendship Lost	1
Benny Can't Play Pool Here Anymore	4
I Love You, Dad	14
Never Say Never	26
This, Too, Shall Pass	36
A Language of Their Own	44
Paint a Little Square	52
Be Humble in Victory	64
Can You Get My Mom Back to Me?	70
We'll Find You the Money	76
Help Me Save the One I Love	84
We Haven't Done This in a Long Time	96
It's Not Easy to Do What You Have to Do	108
A Faith Like Jamie's	114

You Have to Have Love	120
You Don't Have a Tape?	132
Those Dreaded Sand Traps	140
Humility	150
Saying "Hello"—Saying "Goodbye"	158
Attitude Can Change Adversities into Assets	168
"Thank You, Mr. Henry"	180
Most Richly Blessed	196
A Trilogy of Miracles	202
Another Favorite Story to Live By: The Struggle	214
The Greatest Lesson Ever Learned	220
About the Author	230
Diane	231
Chris	232
David	234
Jennifer	235
Jason	236
Henry	238

FOREWORD

Paint a Little Square is about one man's life lived in the midst of miracles. That man, Henry Tews, has been my friend for nearly twenty years. During that time, I have witnessed his incredible achievements of the improbable and the impossible as he followed his dreams and vision with a singular purpose.

Although Henry fondly refers to me as his mentor, we have always shared a passion for serving those less fortunate and a genuine appreciation of each and every human being's place in this world. This bond of compassion has provided us with a wonderful opportunity to grow together personally and fulfill the promise of our divine mission.

As you travel with him through his experiences, you will join countless others whom he has taught to view the events in their own lives from a spiritually higher level. Henry is always provocative and never indifferent, and his stories of enlightenment, inspiration, and empowerment nurture our souls and challenge both our human spirit and intellect.

As a minister, I marvel at his ability to relate his spiritual idealism to the everyday realities of life in such a way that any reader can appreciate his message. Moreover, that message is truly profound, for it speaks of embracing faith, love, vision, and hope—one day at a time—throughout our lives.

Paint a Little Square motivates, stimulates, and inspires our appreciation of who we are. Reading it is an excellent way to spend time in reflection and thought. Share it with a friend or loved one, and you will share the joys of faith and life itself.

—*Rev. Henry Soles*

In addition to being Senior Chaplain for the Chicago Bulls basketball team, Reverend Henry Soles is an award-winning journalist, editor, television personality, community leader, and worldwide motivational speaker.

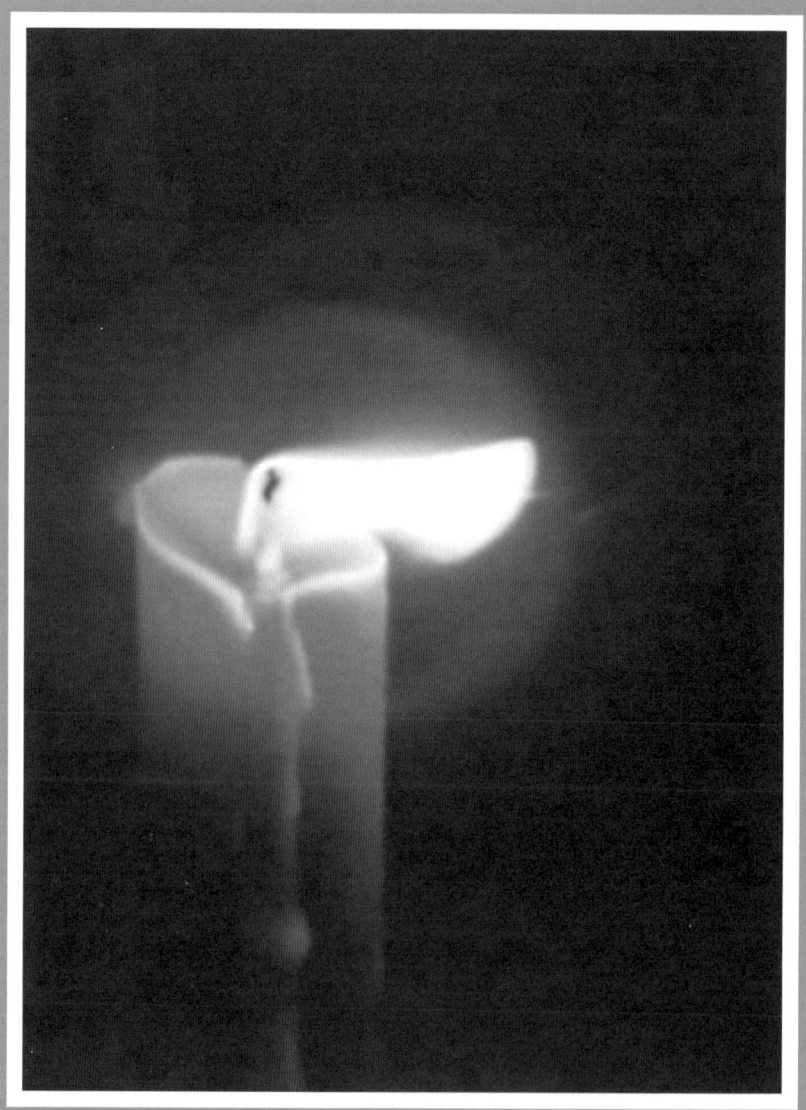

PHOTO BY STEVE McPHETERS

TO A FRIENDSHIP LOST

He moved quickly like the wind, sometimes violently like a tornado. She was like a candle, glowing in the darkness of life. It was inevitable that the two should meet sometime, someplace.

The surge of wind gave resilience to the flame, but the light was in grave danger of being extinguished, so the tornado withdrew. More and more he realized how beautifully the gentle and fragile candle glowed in the darkness even from a great distance. Sometimes for a brief moment, he could sense the glow, and just knowing it was there, he felt her beacon flashing, "All is well."

One day, someone picked up the candle, took it out of the room and shut the door.

2

It was dark…very dark,

and the wind was still…very still.

For it is in the stillness of life that we find life.

It is in the stillness of life that we find serenity.

It seems to me

you lived your life

like a candle in the wind,

Never knowing

who to cling to

when the rain set in.

—Elton John

PHOTO BY STEVE McPHETERS

BENNY CAN'T PLAY POOL HERE ANYMORE

On my ninth birthday in the fall of 1943, my grandparents asked me what I would like to do to celebrate. Thinking that I was quite the man, I tried to think of what was the most adult thing I could do.

Whenever Grandpa had guests, the men would go downstairs into the basement after dinner. They would light up their cigars, pour their brandy or schnapps and play pool. Watchers would sit in large elevated hard oak armchairs. I asked my grandpa if I could bring a friend over to play pool for my birthday. When he agreed, I was very excited.

The following week I brought my friend over to play pool. As we went down to the poolroom, I introduced Benny to my grandparents. Usually my friends and I would be given

6

some cookies and juice, but none was served this time. For a moment I thought this was strange, but I was so excited to play pool with my friend that any question or inquiry about refreshments quickly left my mind. We played for about an hour when Grandpa announced it was time to go. I was very proud that I had been able to share that poolroom with my friend.

The next day my mother told me that Grandpa wanted me to stop by his house on the way home from school. Visiting Grandpa two days in a row was quite unusual. He was the only real father figure I knew, and to me, he was a giant.

He had built a huge concrete company with our name on the trucks and the buildings around Milwaukee. He would go hunting in Canada to kill moose and bring home these huge animals. At home, he would hang them in the back yard from a large beam suspended from the top of the garage. His name, along with Grandma's, was displayed on the bottom of stained glass windows at their church. His presence and power were evident everywhere.

For the second day in a row, I arrived at Grandpa's house and was taken into the living room. When Grandpa was going to have a serious talk he would hold it in the stately living room. Initially, Grandpa asked me a lot of questions about school, free time and friends. He finally asked me whether I was aware that Benny was a Jew. I was very confused as I tried to figure out just what difference that made. Grandpa continued talking about how bad the Jews were and then he said, "Benny can't play pool here any more."

8

Almost sixty years later, I can still feel the pain. I can see myself as that little boy with tears in his eyes standing up to that giant and saying. "If Benny can't play pool here, then neither will I. I will never play pool here again." Grandpa probably thought this was a little boy's threat and was not to be taken seriously.

Years went by. Benny went his way and I went mine. I never told him the story even though our paths would cross occasionally. He grew up to be a very gracious and kind man.

After my hitch in the Army, I returned to Milwaukee and learned that my uncle, aunt and lawyers had legally manipulated me out of my inheritance. With a lot of bitterness and anger, I began a new life, got married, started a family and moved to Illinois.

A number of years had passed when I received a phone call informing me that my grandfather was dying and wanted to see me. I had heard that he had been declared legally incompetent quite some time before and was unable to make decisions regarding his estate and will.

As I stood at his bedside. I could not hold back all the emotions that had been bottled up for years. Lying in the bed was a skeleton of a man whom I remembered to be a giant. Cylinder tanks and breathing tubes were attached to his face. Intravenous feeding lines were in his arms, his eyes were shut, and he was barely breathing. A nurse said, "Dad, Henry's here." His eyes opened, but I could not recognize the man I was looking at. The oxygen mask was removed and he whispered, "Come here." I brought my ear as close as I could to his face and then he said, "I made a horrible mistake. I let them steal your inheritance. I'm so sorry. Can you forgive me?"

I did not want to forgive him. My "justifiable resentment" was the negative force that had fueled my obsessive energy for years. How could I let all of that go with a simple "I'm sorry"? I backed away in shock and anger. He motioned me to come close again.

"They have taken all of the material things I could have given you," he continued, "but one thing they cannot take is my love. I leave you my love," he said. Then, as if his strength were sapped, he closed his eyes. At that time I knew that I had been given an opportunity to free myself from my hate and anger. "Grandpa," I said, "I forgive you. I leave you with my love, also." I could see a smile come on his face as he fell asleep.

I walked out of his room and slowly worked my way down into the dark basement and turned the lights on in the poolroom. A cue stick and ball were lying on the table. I picked up the cue ball and realized that I had not played pool since that time years ago when I played with Benny. I rolled the ball down the table and watched it fall into the pocket, knowing that something amazing had happened to me.

Many years passed while Diane and I built a printing company and raised a family. At age fifty I started an alcohol and substance abuse treatment center called Serenity House. It continues to be recognized as an outstanding facility with great programs.

12

In April of 1997, I had the good fortune to run into Benny again in Milwaukee. We spent some time sharing life stories. I told him about my work with Serenity House and that I had heard he had become a very successful business owner. We reminisced about our childhood and talked about a multitude of nothings. He seemed quite happy just to chat. He invited me to supper, but I had a plane to catch. He asked for my card, we shook hands and parted. Several weeks later I received a donation in the mail.

I wondered, as I held the check, about this kind, gentle and wonderful man. Benny had built a great business empire and had amassed great wealth, respect and success. If my Grandfather were alive today, would he still tell me that "Benny could not play pool here anymore"?

Experience is not what happens to a man;

it is what a man does with what happens to him.

—Aldous Huxley

PHOTO BY STEVE McPHETERS

I LOVE YOU, DAD

My father died as an alcoholic at the age of thirty-three. I was three at the time, and was raised in part by my grandparents. Grandpa was a hard-core, old country German. He found no value in childhood games like baseball, football or basketball. Instead, he taught me how to shoot a rifle and sent me into the orchard to kill birds. At the end of the day, I would be paid for each carcass I presented to him before they were unceremoniously discarded. At the age of ten, I learned to row a boat for hours without ever splashing an oar while Grandpa fished for muskies. Each day I would row the boat hour upon hour while Grandpa fished. When he hooked one I would hand him the thirty-two caliber revolver and watch as he shot the fish. This made it easier to get them into the boat.

Grandpa bred hunting dogs and sometimes the litter had poorly born pups. Those puppies were considered of no value, and I looked on as they were destroyed. Sometimes, it was my responsibility. Looking back at it now, I cannot comprehend how he could have taught a boy of eleven to do that. It was as if the man were totally inhuman. I am convinced that these trained disciplines were designed to remove all aspects of humanity, including love. Feelings and emotions were not allowed around Grandpa.

King was the only real bright spot in my life. He was a springer spaniel, and a great hunting dog. A lot of good moments were spent when Grandpa and I would take him for a walk. Every once in a while he would scare up a rabbit, but King was getting old and would quickly tire of the chase. One day as we were getting ready to go for our walk, Grandpa told me to bring a shovel. We came to a hill sort of overlooking the lake. "This is a beautiful place." Grandpa said as he ordered King to sit. As King obeyed, he took the thirty-two out of his pocket and shot my dog. I was shocked and devastated and began to cry. "Stop crying," Grandpa ordered. "We Tews do not cry. King was getting too old and it was difficult for him to run. Now he won't have any more pain. Bury him and when you are done, come to supper," Grandpa said. I started digging, and when Grandpa was out of sight, I hit the ground and cried. It was dark when I finally got back to the house. "Why are you so late?" Grandma asked. "The ground was hard," I answered. "I think that you're lying," Grandpa said. "For your punishment you can go to bed without any supper!"

The next day I took a small jar and sneaked into the liquor cabinet. I stole a cigar and put some schnapps in the jar. I ran off into the woods, drank the schnapps and started smoking the cigar before I passed out. It was my first experience with liquor. Grandpa found me sometime later, woke me and started yelling at me as I had almost started a forest fire with the burning cigar. After a beating, he dragged me to the boathouse and ordered me to clean it up. I remember feeling hopeless and walked toward the fishing boat. I got in and opened the tackle box and took out his gun. I aimed it at the door, thinking that if Grandpa were gone, I would never be beaten again. Fortunately, I came to my senses quickly. Feeling exhausted, I put the gun away and fell asleep in the boat.

Of course, I was sent directly to my room again that night without supper. I could hear my grandparents talking about sending me to military school. Grandpa felt that they could knock some sense into my head. For me, any place had to be better than where I was. I spent five years in the military academy and without a doubt, it saved my life. My training during my most formative years made me very proficient and I graduated as first sergeant and the corps' best-drilled cadet. I also learned that alcohol could kill feelings and numb human emotions.

After graduation, I spent three years in the army and found that three packs of cigarettes a day and plenty of booze

20

would keep me alive, without having to feel any pain or discomfort. This was my pattern for the next five years while I worked, went to college on the GI Bill, and existed in a rooming house.

In class at night I met the most fantastic woman in the world and married Diane three months later. I was in a big hurry. I am sure that if we had waited any longer, she would have gotten to know the real me and changed her mind. The next five years were a living hell for Diane. We moved to Illinois and had three children. As if the babies weren't enough, she had to deal with a crazy husband who had no feelings, who smoked insanely, and drank himself into an unconscious state every day.

On December 10, 1964, I hit rock bottom and finally called for help. Two men came to me and said what I thought was the most incredible and impossible thing I had ever heard. "As of today, you will no longer have to drink." Thanks to those men, the Twelve Step program and my Higher Power, that statement came true. It has taken me ten years to know who I am, ten more to learn about life, and ten more to know what love is all about. I am still learning how to put it all together today, and find that life's lessons come to us in many different ways.

Some years back another profound event occurred that dramatically changed my life. Diane and I went to college orientation day for our second son, David. We sat with the

22

rest of the parents in a large auditorium and listened to a professor talk about the changing relationship we would be experiencing with our children now that they were in college. He said, "There are only three words that count to your child in college, or in life. What they want to hear, what they must hear, is 'I love you.'"

"Can you say those three words?" he asked. "Okay, now look at your son or daughter and tell them "I love you." For a moment the room was silent and then I could hear hundreds of parents saying, "I love you" to their children. I didn't remember ever saying it before that day. Then the professor told us to never let a telephone call or visit end without telling our child those three words. From then on, our family began the practice of doing just that. I probably didn't understand what it all meant, but I knew that it was a good thing. Diane and all the children did the same, and as the years went by it grew on us.

Four months ago, I had my second heart bypass surgery. Just before I was to go into the operating room, four of my children and my wife Diane were in my room. Diane looked down at me and said, "Why are you crying? We've been married thirty-eight years and I've never seen you cry. Why now?" I looked at her and said, "Because now at this late date in my life, I have finally found out what love is. Now I can see how much I want to live and be a part of your lives. Why did it take so long?" My son David was on his way home from Spain,

24

and I thought of him as I was wheeled down the corridor. I thought about the last time I hugged him and told him that I loved him and felt the tears go away as a smile came to my face.

I fell in and out of consciousness as the sedatives were taking effect. It was as though my thoughts were traveling into space and I was there with David. I could hear myself saying, "I love you Son," and his response, "I love you Dad." I was in complete serenity with the world as I fell asleep.

In everyone's life, at some time,

our inner fire goes out.

It is then burst into flame by an

encounter with another human being.

We should all be thankful for those people

who rekindle the inner spirit.

—Albert Schweitzer

PHOTO BY STEVE McPHETERS

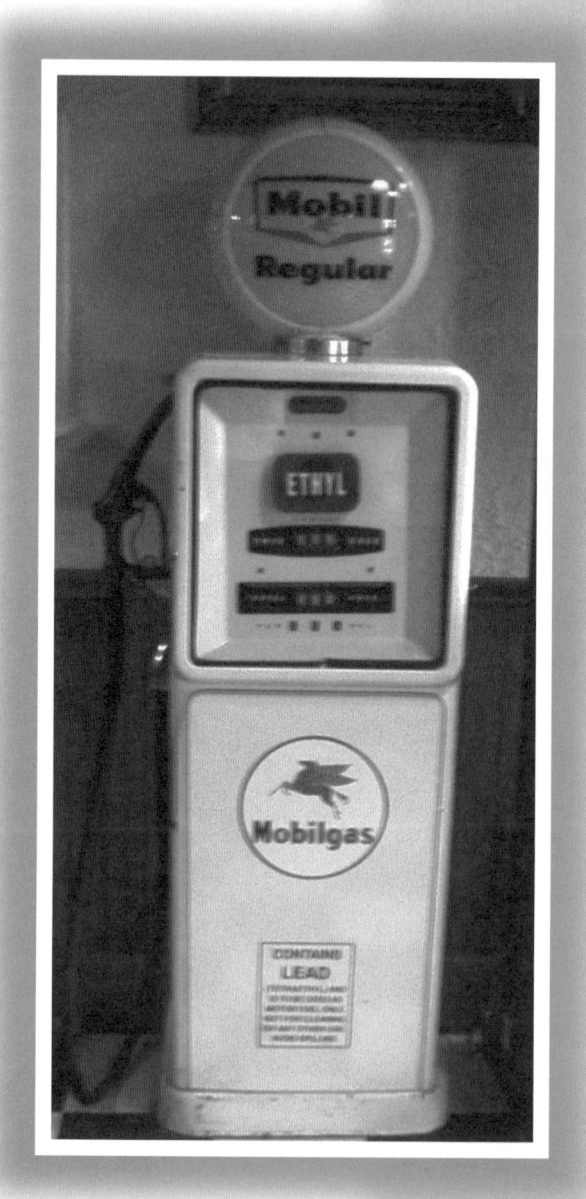

NEVER SAY NEVER

Many wealthy people assume they know the value of life and can judge others. My grandparents were quite wealthy and condemned my poor mother, as much for her poverty as her inability to change their son.

I was three when my father died, with two older sisters, and a younger sister born several weeks after my father's death, leaving my mother alone to raise us. My mother was a good, hard-working woman and a great mom. At the age of sixteen, I told my grandparents I could no longer listen to them calling my mother a murderer. I was promptly disowned. I was given fifty dollars and sent on my way.

28

My mother married another alcoholic, Jim. Like many alcoholics, he was a nice guy one moment and a master manipulator the next. His failure to keep his commitments from a previous marriage always had him on the run, dodging the police, investigators, creditors, and whomever else he owed. The railroad extra gang was a great place for him to disappear. Then his past caught up with Jim again, and he headed to Texas.

I graduated from military school as a First Sergeant, the best-drilled cadet, and I took that job on the railroad extra gang. I saw and experienced things I will never forget, things that were so horrific that they are still vivid in my mind today. Many of those experiences are the foundation for what we are doing at Serenity House today.

The men who worked the track were called "gandy dancers." Approximately one hundred men made up the extra gang, mostly alcoholics or the down-and-outers from the streets in the Midwest. They were hauled to the work site in old passenger cars, and most were too sick to work the first day. They laid in their bunk beds until the bed bug bites drove them out of bed. Against orders, I visited the living quarters. The stench, filth, and bug-infested areas were unbelievable. I asked the railroad extra gang supervisor for help, but he threatened to fire me. They had tried to clean it up, but it was a waste of time. He warned me to stay out and never mention it again.

Most of the men lasted three or four days, and then they would take a discounted advance on their pay. They purchased cigarettes at inflated prices from the railroad commissary, walked to the town tavern, and bartered the cigarettes for cheap wine and cash. They bought bread and high-alcohol automobile additives. They strained the additives through the bread and added this concentrated alcohol to the wine and drank it. It drove them crazy! One fell on the tracks and was killed by a train. The police came and kicked the men on the insteps of their feet. If they moved, they let them lay open to the sun, rain or wind, passed out and oblivious to the world around them. If they didn't move and had no pulse, they called the funeral home to pick them up.

This was too much for me, so I went to a local church and asked the pastor for help. "I've tried to help in the years past, all to no avail. I just wasted my time," the pastor said. "There are so many people who need my help. I can't use my time on those who don't want it."

I promised myself I would never be an alcoholic. I could no longer handle the miserable sights around me so I quit. However, within months I was working side by side with some of these men for ninety-five cents per hour at a cannery. It was hard physical labor, and sometimes I worked over one hundred hours a week. We worked, we drank, and I became a full-blown alcoholic by eighteen years of age, but I sent all my savings to my mother and Jim to bank for me.

After I quit the cannery, I joined the Army and was sent to Europe. By this time, I was drinking heavily and almost received a medical discharge. During my entire military hitch, I sent most of my paycheck home for safekeeping.

After my discharge, I was ready to start a new life. When I arrived home, I discovered that Jim had spent all my savings, except the original $50. My poor mother never knew. I ended up in a slum apartment in Milwaukee, went to Marquette University on the GI Bill, and got a job at a gas station.

Even after all Jim had done to me, he came to the gas station one day for a free fill-up and a handout.

I told him, "No, not only will I not give you gas or money, but I never want to see you or hear from you again. Never!"

After he drove off, I felt bad about what I had said, so I tried to call him. I finally got in touch with my Mom, and she was crying and sounded very upset.

"What's wrong?" I asked.

"Jim's dead," my mother answered.

Jim had died of a heart attack on the way home. My mother had sent him to me for help. They were desperate without a dollar between them. I could not bring myself to ever tell my mother what I had said. I wished I had never said, "Never," and now it was too late. There would be no closure, only pain and regrets. I was drinking heavily then, but there wasn't enough alcohol to numb the feelings or ease the pain.

Recently, while recuperating from my second heart surgery, a concerned friend from Alcoholics Anonymous

34

said, "I suppose now that you have had your second bypass surgery you'll never be able to visit Dairy Queen again!"

With a slight chuckle I answered, "To live without Dairy Queen would be too hard to do, but more importantly, I've learned never to say never."

If you judge people,

you have no time to love them.

—Mother Teresa

PHOTO BY WENDI A. SORENSEN

THIS, TOO, SHALL PASS

When I arrived at AA thirty-three years ago at the age of thirty, I felt like a fish out of water. Most of the "old timers" were twenty years my senior, and although those who brought me to my first meeting were very kind and caring, I felt it was not the place for me. I was full of myself, wallowing in self-pity, denial, and injured pride. I was so compulsive and addictive that I also gave up smoking, cold turkey, on the same day. Some members said I was nuts—probably the best diagnosis I had ever received, and others gave me excuses not to come back. They did not think thirty was old enough to be an alcoholic.

AA was still evolving, and alcoholism was not yet recognized as a disease. A lot of their remedies were in the

38

development stage of trial and error. The commitment to AA was supposed to be total. We were expected to be submerged in their philosophy, or out the door. One member told me, "Relapse is not an option."

As a father of two, with a third on the way, I tried to adapt to AA and survive. We had little or no money. I could not keep a job and my reputation made it impossible for me to find a new one. Our medical bills were beyond payment. We had no insurance and no way to pay a doctor or hospital bills for our third child. I could not see any reason to stay sober. At least when I was drunk, I could go into oblivion and let the rest of the world worry about my problems. The magic elixir was the simple way out.

One night at a meeting I found Ted, one of those "old timers", and told him my story. I guess I was looking for some love, compassion, a hug, or words of encouragement. Instead, after listening to my troubles, he looked at me without any emotion and said, "This, too, shall pass." He walked away. It was brutal. I was in such pain and all he could give me was a cliché. I felt AA had failed me.

I walked the town's streets for hours, and finally returned home. My wife greeted me with, "We have to go to the hospital, the baby is due."

I sat alone in the waiting room. At this moment of the greatest despair of my life, I knelt to pray. It was the first time, and maybe the only time I really prayed. I asked for only one thing. "God, please let me not drink just for today," whatever that day might be. The compulsion to drink and the desire to escape left me immediately, and never returned. I sat back in the lounge chair knowing all was well. Soon after, the doctor came in the room and announced we had a very healthy baby boy, whom we named Christopher.

Shortly after Christopher's birth, I found a good job as a salesman working on commission. One thing I know for certain about alcoholics: if they can stay sober and in a treatment program, they can be the best friends, the best employees, and the best people anyone could meet. We paid our bills, put money in the bank, and bought a new house and car. I finally had nice clothes and money in my pocket.

I went back to that AA meeting and searched for Ted. I told him how great things were going with my house, car, clothes, and money. Again he listened patiently and without a shred of emotion he said, "This, too, shall pass."

My wife and I have been married thirty-seven years, raised four sons and a daughter, have six grandchildren, and built a very successful printing company. Twenty years after my prayer, I founded and built Serenity House. Serenity House is now fifteen years old, with fifty-four clients in the residential program, and over one hundred fifty clients in the non-residential program.

When people come to us with stories of despair, without hope, that old maxim is still true, "This, too, shall pass."

42

But at Serenity House, we also give them a hug and words of hope for the future.

Lessons taught in fear are remembered.

But lessons taught in love are cherished.

—Anonymous

PHOTO BY STEVE McPHETERS

A LANGUAGE OF THEIR OWN

For several years, I had driven to the prison in Joliet on Wednesday nights to carry the message of the Twelve Steps. I had never been incarcerated and had not "walked in their shoes" and yet, I could relate to their loneliness, isolation and fear. Their prison felt similar to the prison I had put myself in during the years I abused alcohol. Suicide attempts during blackouts, the financial despair caused by my liquor bills and loss of income when I failed to show up at work, had put me in a prison far more restrictive than the walls and bars of the prison that I would visit every week.

I felt something very familiar and eerie about the sound of those jail doors as they closed and locked shut behind me on Wednesday nights. Without my having to say anything, the men would top off their coffee, put out their cigarettes, and sit down in an orderly fashion, as talking stopped. The meeting was usually attended by thirty or forty people, most of them lifers or individuals sentenced to long prison terms. Many of them would never see the outside again.

I still remember an inmate named Johnny. At seventy-two, he was forty years my senior. He stood tall, a humble, stately southern man who had been in prison for the past thirty-five years. After serving twenty years, he had been paroled, but was unable to handle life on the outside and returned to the only life he knew as an adult.

Johnny's age-old wisdom and knowledge of the system made him a valuable counsel to me. He shook his head many times as he tried to tell me, "These men have a language of their own. You must learn it if you really want to reach them." Despite his good advice my ego led me to do things my way.

We got to know each other very well and spoke often. He wanted me to learn to be strong and secure in my own self and stressed that my mission was not meant to reinforce my ego, but to provide assistance to the inmates. It was not my message I was sent to carry, but the message of the Twelve Steps. "All the better if the two were the same," Johnny would say.

I recall a dramatically different meeting night when everyone just kept on talking after I entered the room. I walked to the front and waited. After five minutes,

48

I announced that it was time to begin our meeting. At that moment, I met our newest member. He was not only huge in size, but his voice was screaming obscenities as he informed me that nothing would start until he was ready. His vulgarity caught me completely off guard and seemed to permeate the room. My shock was apparent to everyone, especially Johnny who sensed my fear and concern in the situation. Slowly, he walked up to the fellow who was ruling the room and whispered in his ear. The look on the new member's face indicated that a giant revelation had just occurred. The big fellow starting barking commands, "Cigarettes out! No talking! Find a chair and get in it now!" Then, turning to me he, apologized, "Sorry, sometimes we get confused and make mistakes. It will never happen again." He sat in a front chair, and was attentive for the entire meeting.

Not knowing what Johnny whispered in the man's ear was driving me crazy. I cannot recall any other details of the meeting. I continuously focused on what had been said. When the session ended, the big fellow very politely thanked me for coming as he calmly left the room. I saw Johnny walking down that hall and followed him, shouting his name in pursuit. I needed to know what profound thing Johnny had passed on that caused such an immediate reaction. "Johnny, Johnny," I said, my voice quite emotional, "What did you say to that big guy?" "Aw, shucks," Johnny responded, "It was really nothing. I just told him you were on the parole board."

50

My drive home that night was slow and quiet as I mulled the evening over in my mind. Johnny had been right, of course. When trying to communicate with people, it's important to remember that they often come from a different place and may indeed have a language of their own.

Nothing in life is to be feared.

It is only to be understood.

—Marie Curie

PHOTO BY CRAIG WOELFE

PAINT A LITTLE SQUARE

It was a cold, damp October evening in 1986. There was an eerie stillness in the air and the fog was thick. In the darkness, the old building stood out as a monumental obstacle blocking all plans for a pleasant future.

Four months earlier, I had delivered brochures, explaining my dream of building a halfway house and requesting help, to Twelve Step groups. Although they took the brochures, they did not help, quoting tradition. Did they want me to fail as so many had done in the past? They called it an ego trip and said that the other addicts and I would never succeed.

Ninety-five percent of the people who were involved in the project were not addicts; they were friends and family of addicts who believed in the miracles that occurred in halfway houses. For two years, they had supported me as I worked full time on the project. Did these groups just fear having the halfway house in their backyard?

Standing on the hill, a favorite place of mine to meditate, reality hit me. I had no funds or high profile financial organization to support the effort. I knew of no one who could run this project on a volunteer basis and we did not have operating funds to hire someone. The future task seemed impossible for a healthy man let alone one who had just had bypass surgery a little more than a year before.

As I was lost in my thoughts, my friend, Johnny came up to me. He was extremely concerned about my health and my sobriety. "Look," he said, "you have given it a great start and I'm sure Serenity House will make it, but I am concerned about you and if you'll make it. Why not turn it over to someone else?" His parting words were, "We don't want to lose you."

Alone again, I came to the same realization. I could not go on. In the cold, dark, still evening, my prayers seemed to cut through the fog as I asked my Higher Power to release me from my twenty year pledge to start a halfway house. I thought of Jesus and how he must have felt when he was alone and in despair, and I knew of only one place to turn for help.

"Can you help?" I asked and all the problems with the project seemed to disappear. I started walking the site and asked, "What do I do with the barn? How do I dismantle a barn or that huge two-story dilapidated one hundred year-old wooden house with asbestos siding?" As I passed the buildings, it seemed the burdens were lifted and a sense of freedom came over me until I reached the small cottage.

Upon entering the small cottage, the hopelessness and despair seemed to return and close in on me. There is no way this place will be ready for occupancy in December, I thought. The place should have been condemned and torn down. The foul air was stifling and began choking me. I looked at the one light in the cottage that hung from a makeshift extension cord, and the hopelessness overtook me. I got down on my knees, and looking to the heavens said, "You can't ask me to do this."

I was waiting for an answer when a spot on the wall caught my attention. Someone had missed a spot, which was shaped like a square, while painting the wall. Accepting my answer, "Okay," I said, "I can do that. I can paint that little square."

Saturday, three months since I began my heavenly appeal, was to be volunteer day. I had asked people to come to the site and help in any way they could. They told me they would not come and be a part of "Henry's Follies." They walked out of a room when I entered and at restaurants, they left their tables as I attempted to join them. "Come Saturday, if all you want me to do is paint that little square," I told God, "I can do that but nothing more."

A breeze came over the site as I closed the cottage door. The fog had lifted and the lights from the Chicago skyline, more than thirty miles away, shone brightly. It was a beautiful sight and my whole being was filled with happiness and joy. I could do this one simple task—paint a little square.

Saturday morning came. I had arrived at eight-thirty even though I had advised the volunteers to come at ten o'clock. After entering the cottage, I slowly opened the can of paint with optimistic enthusiasm, looking for some divine message. I dipped the brush into the can and painted the square on the wall. Any and all expectations I had were answered in silence as I completed the painting.

With mixed emotions, I found the only chair in the cottage, a rocking chair, and sat down to think. It wouldn't work even if the volunteers did show up, I thought. What I really need is a 'jack of all trades' who could live on site and only need room, board and a stipend to get by. I sat there quietly, rocking back and forth, knowing my dream was coming to an end.

In that silence, it came to me: this is not 'my' halfway house. It was the good Lord's. Not until I was prepared to relinquish all ownership, open my stewardship as testimony to the fact that Serenity House belonged to my Higher Power, and make continued sobriety my only reward would Serenity House become the miracle it was conceived to be. I made that pledge and rested back in the rocking chair totally absent from self and in peace.

There was a knock at the cottage door. Hearing my invitation to come in, a man, looking a little tired but showing a great deal of strength, entered. "I heard you are looking for help," he said, "my name is Warren." "What can you do?"

I asked. "I am a jack of all trades, but mostly I'm a carpenter," he answered. How significant, I thought, He sent me a carpenter. Warren must have seen my face light up but I am not sure he saw the tears in my eyes. "There is one problem though," he continued, "I only have a bike as transportation. Do you think I could stay here and I will work for my room, board and a couple of bucks spending money?" "That is called a stipend," I answered, "and I think that can be arranged." "Great, you've got a deal," Warren said.

We sealed the deal with a handshake and Warren inquired, "What are all those people doing here?" "People, what people?" I asked. Warren pointed to the group of people who had assembled outside the cottage and more were coming by the car and truckload. Some of the people were hauling out trash while others were setting up a place for lunch. I could not believe they had actually come to help.

Now fifteen years later, Serenity House has gone from one person's dream to a highly recognized alcohol and substance abuse treatment center. Thirty-two men and twenty-two women reside in the multiple facilities and over one hundred fifty people are in our outpatient program. We have a staff of twenty-three consisting of interns and volunteers and a half million dollar annual budget.

During a press interview, regarding the new thirty-two bed facility that was opening that fall, a reporter asked me "To what do you owe your success, Henry?" "First," I replied, "all credit goes to my Higher Power, whom I wish to call God, and secondly, to knowing your priorities in life. You don't have to do everything, sometimes all you have to do is paint a little square."

Once the interview had ended, another man asked the reporter to explain my response. "I understand the Higher Power part but the idea that all this started with the painting of a little square, now that is something to think about," the reporter responded as he chuckled and walked away.

Continuous effort—

not strength or intelligence—

is the key to unlocking our potential.

—Liane Cardes

PHOTO BY STEVE McPHETERS

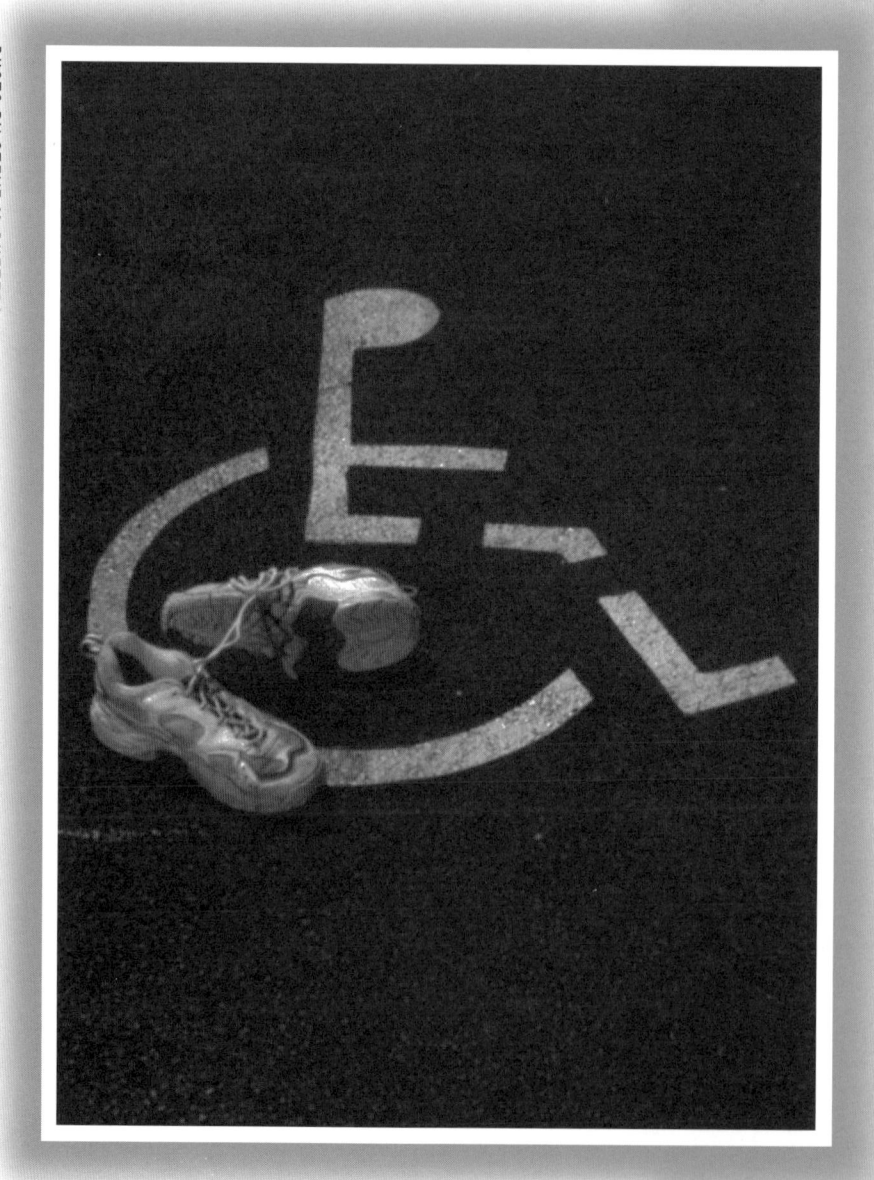

BE HUMBLE IN VICTORY

Some time ago I was doing my normal channel surfing when I was caught up with watching a story unfold at the end of a marathon.

The winner was standing alone at the finish line. The race had been over for some time, but he was still there, with his trophy sitting on the winner's table, surrounded by thousands of discarded cups on the ground. The fact that he was standing alone intrigued me. I knew he was not really alone, as the television crew was still filming him without an announcer or TV person interviewing him. It was as if they were making a still photograph, totally silent.

Then the camera slowly panned to the left, telescoping down the road to an object just coming into view. It was

66

a handicapped fellow in a wheelchair. He appeared to be re-energized when he saw the finish line, the TV cameras, and the winner, his friend. Then people started to appear from everywhere. His momentum increased. I could feel every working muscle in his body propel the wheelchair forward. The crowd started to cheer and people applauded as he crossed the finish line.

The winner walked up to him with his own trophy in hand. He gave him a hug and handed him his trophy. They embraced again as tears rolled down their faces. The sound of the crowd was overwhelming. The man in the wheelchair raised his hand. His friend asked for silence as the TV microphones and cameras moved in closer.

He thanked them all for waiting for him, as it had been many hours since the race had ended. He spoke of life and became quite philosophical. He said, "You know we are motivated to excel in everything. Great football coaches have been quoted as saying there is no such thing as having anything but first place as our objective. Second place is not an option. Excel in everything, always going for the top, the best—in sports, in work, in life. It is as if that is all there is supposed to be in life, but that is not life."

He continued, "The times when we are victorious are the times when we must first consider those who lost. We must remember how we felt when we lost and how incredibly wonderful it felt when the victors came by and shook our hand.

68

The first thing we must remember in this human race is to always be humble in victory. Secondly, it is impossible to consider the fact that we will never lose. That is not a reality and yet it is how we handle that loss which will make all the difference. Be gracious in defeat.

"But what is most significant of all is that all of us be given a chance. Sure, we may never be able to hit a home run. It just might be we may never be able to hit the ball, but we all deserve the right to try. Just as important, is that once given the chance, we are grateful. Today you gave me a chance, and I'll never forget you. Thank you."

If you think you are beaten, you are.
If you think you dare not, you don't.
If you like to win, but you think you can't,
It's almost a cinch you won't.

If you think you'll lose, you've lost.
For out in the world we find
Success begins with a fellow's will.
It's all in the state of mind.

If you think you are outclassed, you are.
You've got to think high to rise.
You've got to be sure of yourself before
You can ever win a prize.

Life's battles don't always go
To the stronger or faster man,
But sooner or later the man who wins
Is the one who thinks he can.

—Walter D. Wintle

PHOTO BY STEVE McPHETERS

CAN YOU GET MY MOM BACK TO ME?

Each week as I do my customary walk of the grounds, it is not rare for me to see staff, clients, guests and sponsors talking and visiting with each other at the picnic tables. However this day, I saw a little boy, baseball cap backwards, sitting alone holding his head in his hands at a picnic table near the women's residence.

As I drew closer, I wondered what I should say to this little boy? He saw me coming and raised his head; he wiped the tears from his eyes before looking at me.

"Hi," I said, while sitting down at the picnic table, "My name is Mr. Tews, what is your name?" "Bobby," he said, choked up and holding back tears. "I'm the director here, Bobby. Can I help you?" I responded.

"Can you get my Mom back to me?" Bobby asked. "My Dad, little sister, and me need her real bad. You see, my Mom is in that house right now talking with a counselor who said she is going to have to stay here for a couple a months if she wants to get better. Can you help my Mom get better and come back home to us?"

"Bobby, we will try," I answered. "There are no guarantees, but there is one thing I do know for sure." "What's that?" Bobby asked. Reaching into my pocket, I took out the Serenity House medallion key ring that is always there. "On this coin, Bobby, is a saying that I have used for over 34 years every time I have to face a tough situation like you have right now."

"God, grant me the serenity to accept

the things I cannot change, the courage to change

the things I can, and the wisdom to know the difference."

"I promise, that if you read this whenever you have a problem, you'll find the answer," I said. "Thank you," Bobby answered as he put the medallion in his pocket. Then he got up and walked towards his parents as they came out of the house. His Mom took her bags out of the car, gave them all one more hug and a kiss, and Bobby turned to me and waved good-bye as the family drove away.

In the course of a year, hundreds of people go through our treatment programs and it is very difficult to keep track of them all. So, when I heard a little boy call my name at the annual picnic, I didn't realize who it was.

"I'm Bobby," he said with his familiar baseball cap on backwards. "I want to thank you for giving me back my Mom. My Dad and little sister are here too," he said as he pointed to his family. "That's great," I answered, and Bobby replied, "Could you do me a favor?" "Sure, I'll try," I answered. "I would like to give my little sister one of those coins. Do you have another one?" he asked. "Sure," I answered as I took one out of my pocket and handed it to him. "You won't have to read it to her," he said. "I can do that," and he started to walk away toward his family. Then he stopped, grabbed the bill of his cap and turned it around to face forward like mine. He turned around, smiled and waved to me. "Thank you," he shouted, and turned back toward his family.

I suddenly felt a tear coming to my eyes. This is what it is all about, I thought. This is what it is all about.

The purpose of human life

is to serve

and to show compassion

and the will to help others.

—Albert Schweitzer

PHOTO BY STEVE McPHETERS

WE'LL FIND YOU THE MONEY

THE FOURTH OF JULY WEEKEND WAS NEVER VERY popular with me. It just so happened this one in 1987 was the fifty-year anniversary of my father's death and four years from the date my mother had passed away. Those incidents have caused me to exercise caution during this holiday weekend ever since. When I pulled away from the stoplight into heavy traffic, I saw a small white car traveling toward me at an enormous rate of speed. I braced myself for a collision as everything went dark. I awoke to someone shouting, "Do you want some help out of there?" Without comprehending the gravity of what had just happened, I instinctively answered, "Yes." The force of the impact had put the steering wheel into the driver's seat and shattered most of the van windows, covering me with glass.

A McDonald's restaurant was under construction nearby. A builder's trailer was sitting next to the highway, where fifteen or twenty people were standing in line awaiting employment interviews. If I had not been in that exact place, at that exact time, the white car might have crashed into the trailer and the large group of people. I staggered to the trailer and I called my son, Chris, and told him about the accident. I assured him that I was all right with the exception of some cuts and bruises, but expressed concern for the driver of the other car. I told him that I was heading to a hospital and would call him from there. As happens in the midst of confusion, my paperwork was inadvertently placed on the stretcher of the other accident victim. An announcement of the fatal accident was broadcast on the local radio station with my name given as the deceased. Upon their arrival at the hospital, my family was immediately ushered into the chapel. The chaplain, whom I had known through my AA work at the facility, consoled my family and advised them that I was on life support. "Not my Dad," Christopher said. "He called me, I spoke to him, and he's okay." After further investigation, the hospital apologized for their grievous error and directed my family to where I'd been taken.

While lying in the emergency room, I had an opportunity to reflect about my family and work at Serenity House. My thoughts were interrupted when I became aware that a woman was standing over me. Having heard the radio announcement, she quickly calculated that if I were alive, her husband had to be dead. She began beating at me, while yelling, "You murderer, you killed my husband." I leapt off the table, bleeding shirt and all, and ran out of the emergency room door. I continued running outside, down the wheelchair ramp. As fate would have it, my family had just arrived and I ran toward them in a state of hysteria. After we all calmed down and I was able to explain the series of errors and events that had taken place, we went back into the emergency room. The doctors and nurses finished patching me up, and with my headband, bandages and arm in a sling, I left the hospital looking like a battlefield casualty.

Although in pain, I was able to attend a very important Serenity House meeting the following day at the County Funding Committee that would determine the future growth of Serenity House. The committee members truly believed in

Serenity House, but due to limited funds, were prepared to deny my request for additional funding. Prior to the start of the meeting, a buzz began to circle the room as members began repeating the radio announcement heard by some the day before. Some of the people in attendance were good friends of mine and began dealing with their grief. You can imagine their shock, when I walked into the conference room at the time the meeting was to begin. With my headband, my left arm bandaged and in a sling, the right hand bandaged, I must have looked like an apparition dressed in a suit and tie as I took a seat in the back of the room. I looked to the front and saw that the committee chairperson, whom I had known for a long time, was teary-eyed. To this day I can still see the mix of emotions in that room as people began to notice me.

82

The committee seemed bewildered, not really knowing how to handle their changing emotions. My name was called, as I was first on the agenda. I moved to the front of the room and sat in a lone chair opposite the committee members seated at a long table. Now, fully composed, the committee leader looked at me, then looked to the members on her right and left. "Give him the money," she said to the members on the right. And again, she said, "Give him the money," to the members on the left. She looked at me with a subdued smile and a small tear in her eye and said, "We'll find you the money."

Never let defeat have the last word.

—*Anonymous*

PHOTO BY STEVE McPHETERS

HELP ME SAVE THE ONE I LOVE

LET ME BEGIN BY SAYING THAT ALCOHOLICS AND addicts come in all sizes and shapes; all races, colors, creeds; young and old, rich and poor, men and women, brilliant and less educated. One fact is true: once an addict or an alcoholic, always an addict or an alcoholic. Without the drugs and alcohol, and on a program of sobriety and behavioral change, these men and women can be the finest people, the most professional employees you will ever meet. They are the most loyal friends and greatest champions. They have the ability to show immeasurable love and compassion as spouses, parents or children. They are very valuable, worthwhile and good people.

One of the most difficult or seemingly impossible requests made upon those in the human service world working with addicts is, "Please, can you help me save my child?"

Parents try to negotiate, but in most cases, they have neither the knowledge nor experience to spar with an addict. An addict does not possess the ability to think rationally. That's the reason Twelve Step groups like AA are so successful; recovering addicts understand that the addict is mono-optic, seeing only him or herself. An addict is crisis-motivated; always in a crisis or causing one. They love being the center of attention. They become a Dr. Jekyll or Mr. Hyde, a transformation most rational people will never understand. The addict will place those that care about them in a position that will undermine any assistance offered. Addiction eventually becomes a family disease or illness. Often, it seems that only the addict will survive.

The addict never learns to face the realities of life, since he or she usually begins using drugs for self-medication at an early age. To put it more simply, addicts never "grow up."

Eventually, there may be a moment of truth, or crisis of such proportions that an intervention is forced upon them. Often, those who have been most insistent that they shape up become the enablers and sympathize with the insanity of the situation. Instead of using the event as a motivational force, demanding behavioral change, loved ones can become drawn into the whirlpool of crisis-motivated self-indulgence and succumb, once again, to the whims of the addict. The behavior of addicts never changes; they leave in their wake one tragedy after another.

Some of the following information may seem too simple to be profound. For example, do you know why alcoholics drink? They drink because they want to, until they get to the point where they have to, in order to lead a somewhat normal life. All of the books by professionals contain one common truth: an addict's compulsive behavior will indicate whether he or she is working toward not using or wanting to use. The relapse takes place long before the first drug or drink is picked up. A life of sobriety is a constant commitment to maintaining one's behavior, a behavior that is consistent with a desire not to drink or use. The secret ingredient that makes AA work so profoundly is that addicts understand addicts. Those who have worked the program for a long time are in constant transition and behavioral change—a behavioral change directed toward not wanting to use.

Those who are not addicts are frustrated and disillusioned. They struggle to understand, constantly asking why. One of the major credos in working or living with addicts, is this: Never give them a break, give them an alternative. If they want fifty dollars for food, go with them and buy it. Never give an addict or drunk money. Do not get into a shouting match or verbal exchange because no one will ever win.

Often, "tough love" is difficult to express and harder yet to experience. It is much easier to give in to an addict than to demand and wait for change. The addict will constantly test those who care about him or her. In reality, it should be the other way around. The addict needs to be aware that for every irresponsible act, there will be a consequence. Those that are not able to be tough are destined to become caretakers and enablers.

A parent once told me, "My son says if I try to make him stop using, he will run away from home or kill himself." Certainly, these possibilities are very serious. First, a parent must get professional help immediately whenever a child uses suicidal statements as threats. The second problem of running away may indicate the need for a good treatment program. They must stop using, as there are no other options. In time, their drug use will destroy them. Why waste time? In 33 years of working with addicts, I have never seen life get better while an addict is using and when those around them don't learn how to say "No!"

One of my children threatened to do some of the same things. My response was to put all of his personal possessions on the front porch, take his car and see what he would do, or give him the option to go to a treatment center. Everyone was highly emotional, and could not understand my cruelty. When we got to the treatment center the counselor said I had to learn to detach and let go. My immediate reaction was anger. It is not possible to detach from your children. Caretakers and enablers find many excuses for inappropriate action. If my child, family member or friend had a broken arm, I would quickly turn them over to a doctor for care, but

I could never totally detach from them. I would always be concerned about how their health was progressing. I have learned that I must let go. My son has now been clean and sober for over ten years, due to some great AA support, a strong spiritual commitment, and a family that knows without a doubt that we must all love each other and live one day at a time.

Another course of action is to be well informed. Whether cancer, heart disease, or alcoholism—they don't have to be fatal. Go to Alanon or Family Anonymous. Call AA and ask for guidance. Do not do it alone. Alanon will help you realize that you are powerless over the using alcoholic.

The church can also be a source of spiritual guidance and assistance if it is understood that addiction is a disease, not a moral deficiency. Most people recall a sort of spiritual awakening prior to seeing the truth. I will never underestimate the intervention of the Higher Power.

AA open meetings can provide attendees with basic pieces of information, which are helpful in bringing the situation into focus. Some of you who have lost a child or a friend or a family member to addiction may read this and think, "Maybe had I known that, the outcome could have been different." Over the years, many people have come to me and said, "Thanks for saving my loved one." I respond by stating that I cannot take credit for saving anyone or for his or her success. If I do, then I must also accept the responsibility for their failures, and that would be a burden too great to carry.

94

The using addict or alcoholic is 'self-will running riot.' They are uncontrollable. We allow their insane actions to place a burden of guilt on others. However, please don't ever forget that these are good people who have an addiction. They will be different people when they are clean and sober—when their true personality and potential shows.

Courage doesn't always roar.

Sometimes courage is the little voice

at the end of the day that says

I'll try again tomorrow.

—Mary Anne Ramacher

PHOTO BY STEVE McPHETERS

WE HAVEN'T DONE THIS IN A LONG TIME

THE SUREST WAY I KNOW FOR SOMEONE TO GET CLOSE to his or her Higher Power is to take the bus from the Mexican International Airport to downtown Acapulco. Winding down those narrow mountain roads with the windows and door propped open for ventilation, is truly a spiritual awakening.

I've always been amazed by the pride and beauty of the Mexican people. I am in amazement when beautiful children emerge from their dirt floor houses in clean white clothes on their way to Sunday mass. Pride is a large part of the Mexican heritage and my wife and I experienced a great example during a recent trip.

Each evening in our hotel lobby, the bell captain announced with dignity and a loud voice, in his best English, the destination for guests in the waiting taxis. I was stuck with a dilemma. My wife, Diane, and I had tried to find a local AA meeting without success. I decided to quietly get a cab to take me to an AA meeting. As the people stood in line nearby, I tried to explain to the captain that I wished "to quietly find an AA meeting." Our conversation was constantly interrupted by his vocal announcement of departures. "Two persons for Café Royal. A party of four for Club Aztec. A party of three for Club Acapulco by the Sea." Eventually, he loudly announced, "One person for Alcoholics Anonymous."

Finally, I was off, safely in a cab to an AA meeting. I assumed the fellow who drove the cab must have been a relative of the airport bus driver, as we went in and out of dark back streets. I frequently questioned him, "Alcoholics

Anonymous?" and he always answered "Si." We made one last heart stopping turn, and I saw a neon sign glaring out on a street of total darkness, flashing "Alcoholics Anonymous." I could not believe those flashing lights. I think I doubled his fare with the tip, I was so relieved to still be alive.

The building was an infirmary. Inside a fellow was lying on a cot. His leg had been amputated at the knee, and bloodied bandages covered the surgical end. Another fellow used an old fashioned bug spray-can to spray all the far-away corners, which sent all the roaches to our side. The host only spoke Spanish and I only spoke English, but he gave me a cup, and showed me a seat. It was an aisle seat next to a fellow wearing a red bandana, with long, highly polished, sharply pointed fingernails. A mangy old mongrel came and laid down next to me. He, too, wore a red bandana around his neck. Every time I moved as if to leave, the dog sat up and growled. When I stopped moving, he laid back down. "Old Pointed Nails" said something in Spanish, pointed to my empty cup, took it and departed. He returned with a cup of heavy black coffee adulterated with chicory. It tasted very bitter. He would look at me and smile, I would sip and move a little, and the dog would sit up and growl. It was insanity.

The speaker's tone of voice and body language indicated that all the troubles and trials of mankind were on his shoulders. He spoke tearfully and his voice was often choked. I did not understand a word but understood that he was talking about a very painful time in his life. Somehow, I felt I had been there. Suddenly, his whole body stood erect, and his chest jumped right out. His voice was clear and direct. Then he looked at all of us in the audience, paused, and said, "Alcoholics Anonymous." He spoke fifteen more minutes and I felt I knew every word, and had lived every past moment with him. The audience applauded when he finished.

To be polite, I finished the stuff they passed off as coffee, and started to move. The dog sat up and growled, and "Old Painted Nails" smiled and took my cup. In broken English, he told me there would be three more speakers and he would get me more coffee. I sat for two more hours, only understanding "Alcoholics Anonymous," which created a transfiguration in every speaker. At the end of the meeting they passed a basket, and in gratitude of a moving experience, I was very generous. A fellow came up to me, who first spoke in Spanish and then switching to English, thanked me for the contribution. In a startled voice he asked, "You don't know any Spanish, and you sat here two hours? We are celebrating our third anniversary on Sunday. Would you please come back?"

I promised I would and departed. As I walked down the hill, I could see the beautiful skyline of lights. The night was so clear that I could even see the lanterns on the fishermen's boats in Acapulco Bay. I felt born again and uplifted by the wonderful scenery.

On Sunday, my wife, Diane, good soul that she is, agreed to go with me in spite of all the stories I had told her. The bell captain again, announced the festive destinations of fellow guests, and this time he loudly emphasized, "Two for AA," as if I had found a new convert. I am certain the cab ride took us through downtown Acapulco at least twice. As before, each time I said "Alcoholics Anonymous," the driver would say, "Si," and a few more words I did not understand. Maybe that was good on a Sunday morning. Maybe it was the Lord's plan to build up the anticipation.

When we turned the corner and saw those flashing neon lights, "Alcoholics Anonymous" in full display, it was memorable. This time, however, music was being played. Everyone, adults and children alike, were dressed in their finest clean whites and colors bright. They danced and sang in a festive mood. They celebrated their third annual AA meeting with joy that would make the founders of AA very proud.

The leader, Joseph, spotted me immediately. The greetings from everyone were very warm. The sun was shining on a perfect day and the cool breeze carried the aroma of a Mexican buffet that equaled, if not exceeded, the most elegant banquet. Reality returned when the fellow with long pointed fingernails and red bandana handed me a cup of coffee full to the brim. That ratty old mongrel with matching bandana growled a little and leaned up against me. I felt as if every flea in Mexico was moving to a new home instantly. Joseph went over to the band and they started a drum roll. He escorted Diane and me to a small hastily set-up stage. The drum roll stopped and he spoke to the audience. We were the only Americans to have ever come to their meeting. What I thought was a very small offering at the AA meeting was really a sizeable donation to them. Joseph reached down behind a chair and brought up a very thin wooden board. It was highly polished with words burnt into the surface. Then, with the fanfare of their group's musicians, he announced that in honor of their third anniversary I was being presented with a plaque. It was beautiful and I choked up as he read the words inscribed in Spanish, and then, translated for me in English.

THE PRAYER OF ST. FRANCIS
O Lord, make me an instrument of Thy Peace!
Where there is hatred, let me sow love;
Where there is injury, pardon;
Where there is discord, harmony;
Where there is error, truth;
Where there is doubt, faith;
Where there is despair, hope;
Where there is darkness, light; and
Where there is sorrow, joy.
Oh Divine Master, grant that I may not so much seek
To be consoled as to console;
To be understood as to understand;
To be loved, as to love.
For it is in giving that we receive;
It is in pardoning that we are pardoned;
And it is in dying that we are born to Eternal Life.

When he concluded, the band played again and the people clapped. The festivities continued and we rejoined the crowd. People shook my hand and patted me on the back saying, "Gracias." After we said goodbye to Joseph, we walked down the hill to our hotel a few miles away. Diane talked about the beauty of family and friends and the simplicity of life. We were full of joy, life, and love. I held the plaque in my left hand and my right hand held Diane's. As we walked, I thought, "We haven't done this for a long time."

If you want one year of prosperity, grow grain.

If you want ten years of prosperity, grow trees.

If you want one hundred years of prosperity, grow people.

—Chinese Proverb

PHOTO BY STEVE McPHETERS

IT'S NOT EASY TO DO WHAT YOU HAVE TO DO, TO BE WHAT YOU WANT TO BE

It was a beautiful fall afternoon at Serenity House, located thirty miles west of Chicago, Illinois. The trees were in their full fall colors and they were beautiful. A cool brisk wind was like a wake-up call after my heavy lunch. I had a quick step to my walk as I headed to the main door.

I noticed someone sitting in the vestibule, which was not uncommon, but something did not look quite right. The man was in his late seventies and very disheveled. His clothes were all wrinkled as if he'd slept in them for some time, and he badly needed a bath and a shave. He just sat, looking down at the floor.

When I introduced myself and held out my hand, he lifted his head and grasped my hand. There were tears in his eyes as he looked at me. "Can I help you?" I asked. He responded, "I don't know." He had come without an appointment intending to see a counselor, wanting to know how he could enter the program at Serenity House.

I invited him into my office and offered him a cup of coffee, but quickly realized he needed much more than that. I offered him a shower and afterward took him to the donated clothing closet. Within an hour he looked like a new man, completely transformed, and he accepted my invitation to stay for supper. While we waited, he began to relate the events of his life, which I could easily relate to periods and similar occurrences in mine. One condition had always remained constant. Whenever he faced a time that required making a serious decision, he put himself into a position that compromised his sobriety. More times than not he got drunk. Every time he did this, he added another layer of disguise and denial. Eventually he no longer knew himself.

Not disclosing that I, too, had faced these moments in time and had experienced difficulty in following the program when making decisions, I sat there and listened, constantly saying to myself, "There, but for the grace of God, go I."

We talked about family, about friends, life and the world in general as addicts often do. When we talked about his friends, family, and children and how they no longer wanted him around, I was struck by how different my life was from his now. I have wonderful memories of moments spent with my family and friends. He spoke of marriages that ended in divorce and I thought of my wife, Diane, how we were planning a trip to Paris to celebrate our forty years together.

    He had supper with the men of the halfway house. He promised to come back the following day. I never saw or heard from him again, but I will never forget his parting words. "You know Henry," he had said, "It's not easy to do what you have to do, to be what you want to be. With your help and the help of my Higher Power, I promise to try to do what I have to do, to be what I want to be."

A word of encouragement during failure is worth more than a whole book of praises after a success.

—Anonymous

PHOTO BY STEVE McPHETERS

A FAITH LIKE JAMIE'S

SOME WEEKS AGO, MY WIFE AND I WENT TO VISIT OUR son Jason, daughter-in-law Michele, and grandchildren David and Jamie. After arriving at their home, Jason and I talked as he prepared to go fishing and the women were getting ready to take David for a walk. In the midst of all the confusion, I did not realize that the women were expecting me to watch Jamie while they were gone.

Everyone left and I looked at Jamie, a few months old, sleeping unaware of all that was happening around her. Then suddenly it struck me that I was entrusted with Jamie's well-being and I felt more helpless than she was. What will I do if she wakes up? Who should I call if there is an emergency? Did my wife have her beeper with her?

What I was really asking myself was, could I be kind, gentle, considerate, loving and responsible enough to take care of her? During the days that I drank, just the opposite was said about me. There Jamie lay so peaceful and serene; it was hard for me to imagine anyone so much in concert with the world. Those are feelings most addicts never feel except, of course, when they are lost in their world of alcohol and drugs.

The recovering addict, like little Jamie, must begin a new life. We do not choose this new existence but we know that we are helpless and must begin to trust more freely. We must learn to put our faith not only in others and ourselves but also in a power greater than ourselves. We need people to guide us along the way like a mother or father or grandparents. The main thing is that we cannot do it alone and trust is an important part of a relationship.

We must make this new life an adventure of seeing our new hopes and dreams become reality. Too often, we find out, the goals we set are too great for us to obtain at that period of our lives. We fail in achieving our goals and that failure has a negative effect on our self-esteem. Low self-esteem fuels the insanity and replaces the serenity. We are now in a place with no balance or boundaries. Truth is gone and we feel trapped. We convince ourselves that the only serenity we will ever find is in using drugs or alcohol.

How did we let ourselves drift off the road to recovery? Is it that we did not follow the rules of the road? The road to recovery is traveled every day by millions of people. Through a Twelve Step program, they are able to cut a trail through the dark wilderness and step back into the light. Follow the road that others have paved for you and you will discover the best is yet to come. Millions stand today and give testimony that it does work.

If you are one of the fortunate ones to have made it out of the dark wilderness and now take on the responsibility of guardian, wear your responsibility proudly. You have been entrusted with a gift that only a few are given. Find a quiet place where you can be by yourself, sit back and take a moment of serenity, having a faith like Jamie's.

*If one advances confidently
in the direction of his dreams,
and endeavors to live the life
which he has imagined,
he will meet with a success
unexpected in common hours.*

—Henry David Thoreau

PHOTO BY JEFFREY LANGLOIS

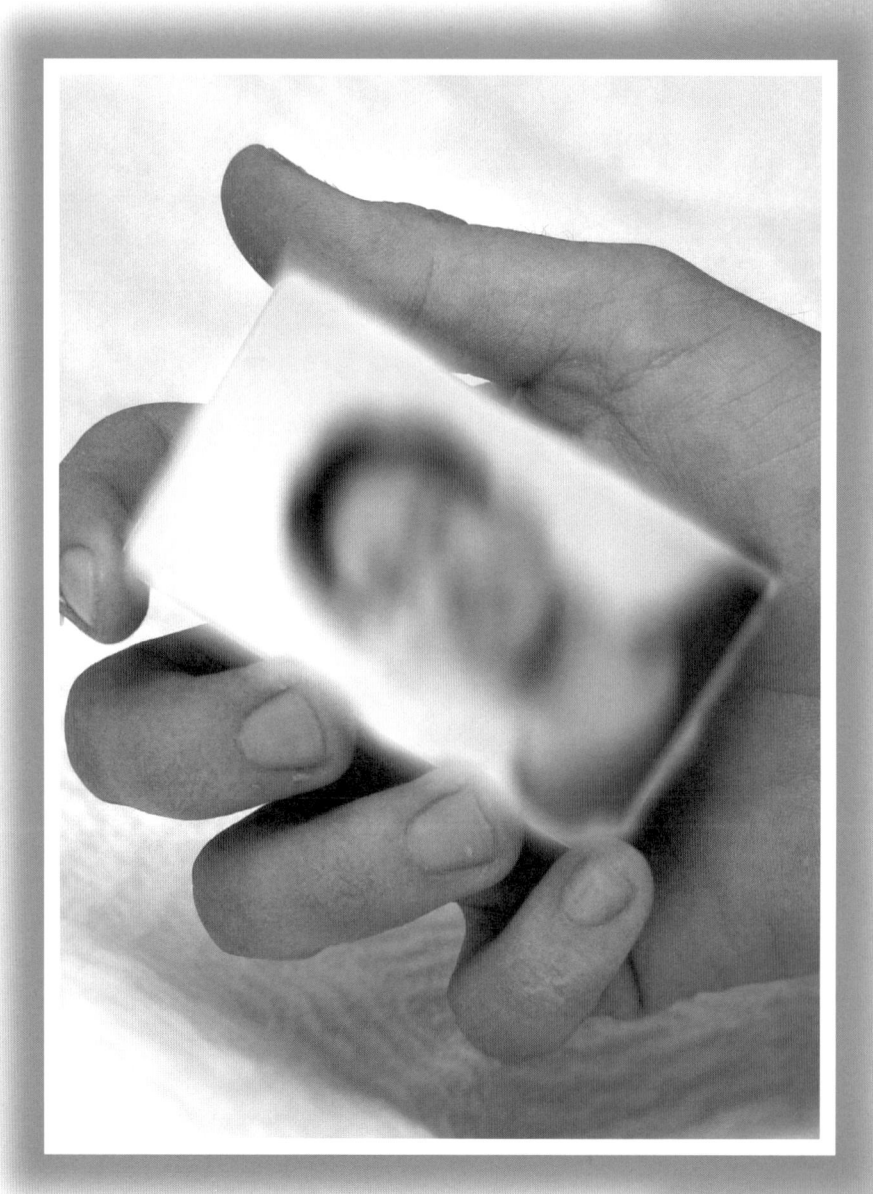

YOU HAVE TO HAVE LOVE

It started as just a normal evening in the men's halfway house, if there is such a thing. The clients were returning home from work, getting ready for supper in a very limited time frame. Things were unusually hectic, but the men had learned to work with it for the most part. This night would be dramatically different.

Roger was a well-groomed, articulate thirty-year-old black male. He had picked this evening in this tight time frame to make a self-disclosure on his own without counsel. He told his three roommates that he was gay. This occurred about the time that Ernie, a white male about twenty-nine years old, was taking off his shirt and getting ready to take a shower, displaying a very distinctive tattoo—KKK. Ernie said some nasty things. It got worse, as Roger added that he was also HIV positive. Ernie kept up his obscenities, as the other two roommates stood there in shock.

Ernie headed to the shower; Roger tried to explain his purpose to the other roommates to no avail and left for the washroom. In those days we did not have the thermo controls on the showers and one could not flush the toilet while someone was showering. Roger did and Ernie was in the shower. He came out screaming and saw Roger, knowing he was the cause, just let out every bit of verbal abuse he had learned while in the correctional world. Roger's verbal platitudes made Ernie's well-tuned muscular frame flex to such a point, everyone present imagined some serious bodily harm would follow. Some of those who had been drawn to the verbal tirade came running to me to intervene.

The outbursts were so vocal and loud that I was already on the way. Upon arriving, I directed Roger and Ernie to get ready for supper, but to see me before they sat down to eat. I asked the other men to explain what happened.

In my office, both Roger and Ernie had their own version of the story. When they were finished I asked them to forgive each other, shake hands and make up. "I'll never shake that gay nigger's hand," Ernie said.

"He's far too ignorant to understand anything. Why should I make up when I did nothing wrong?" Roger responded.

"Then you both need to pack your bags after supper and leave Serenity House." I said. 'If you need assistance or transportation, I'll help you out."

They left my office and I went to supper, returning to my office later to do some paperwork. There was a knock on my door and a group of clients came in. They were petitioning me to reconsider my directive and give the two men a second chance.

"Would you call everyone together in the lounge," I asked. "I will be there in five minutes."

When they were all gathered I addressed them, saying "You are saying that I am discharging Roger and Ernie because one is a gay black man and the other acts like a bigoted ex-con, but that's not true. To live in a community, you must have one ingredient that lives within you every day. You have to have love."

I then read the following:

If I had the gift of being able to speak in other languages without learning them, and could speak in every language there is in all of heaven and earth, but didn't love others, I would only be making noise. If I had the gift of prophesy and knew all about what is going to happen in the future, knew everything about everything, but didn't love others, what good would it do? Even if I had the gift of faith so that I could speak to a mountain and make it move, I would still be worth nothing at all without love. If I gave everything I have to poor people, and if I were burned alive for preaching the Gospel but didn't love others, it would be of no value whatever.

Love is very patient and kind, never jealous or envious, never boastful or proud, never haughty or selfish or rude. Love does not demand its own way. It is not irritable or touchy. It does not hold grudges and will hardly even notice when others do it wrong.

It is never about injustice, but rejoices whenever truth wins out. If you love someone you will be loyal to him no matter what the cost. You will always believe in him, always expect the best of him, and always stand your ground in defending him.

All the special gifts and powers from God will someday come to an end, but love goes on forever. Someday prophecy, and speaking in unknown languages, and special knowledge—these gifts will disappear.

Now we know so little, even with our special gifts,

and the preaching of those most gifted is still so poor. But when we have been made perfect and complete, then the need for these inadequate special gifts will come to an end, and they will disappear.

It's like this: when I was a child I spoke and thought and reasoned as a child does. But when I became a man my thoughts grew far beyond those of my childhood, and now I have put away childish things. In the same way, we can see and understand only a little bit about God now, as if we were peering at his reflection in a poor mirror; but someday we are going to see Him in His completeness, face to face. Now all that I know is hazy and blurred, but then I will see everything clearly, just as clearly as God sees into my heart right now.

There are three things that remain the same—faith, hope, and love—and the greatest of these is love.

1 Corinthians 13: 1–11

I had made copies of this text from the Bible and handed them out. "Let's read this." Then I asked, "Now how many of you are going to try to follow what the Apostle Paul wrote?"

Ernie said, "If I leave here I go back to jail. I can't go back to jail. I will do anything not to go back to jail."

Roger followed, "If I leave here I will surely die. This is my last chance. I'll try anything to stay."

"Well, the first factor of Love is for the two of you to forgive each other and shake hands." As I saw them struggle with their pain at that moment I realized that here the miracle of Serenity House would be tested. Roger broke the deadly silence first by saying he was sorry. Ernie quickly said the same. The two shook hands. The other clients applauded and congratulated them, also shaking their hands.

As the months followed, I saw them become really close friends. One day I saw the bandages on Ernie's shoulder. He had gone to the hospital to have his KKK tattoo removed. The miracles of Serenity House were working in ways I could not believe.

Then one day, I was walking into the recreation room where Roger and Ernie played a lot of Ping-Pong with each other. This was to be their last game. Ernie was leaving. When they tied at twenty, they quit. Neither wanted to beat the other. They gave each other a hug.

"I love ya man," said Ernie.

"I love ya too," followed Roger.

We all had tears in our eyes as Ernie left the room. Roger and I stood in silence, and then Roger said, "I'll miss him."

"You're leaving soon also," I responded. "We will miss both of you."

Months passed and we were looking for individuals to give their testimonials at our annual banquet. "What about Ernie and Roger?" the staff inquired.

Roger could make it, but Ernie had to work second shift that night. "And besides," he said, "I don't have a suit." He insisted he couldn't go without a suit despite my continually telling him that he didn't need one. Ernie said he was sorry, but he just couldn't make it.

The banquet evening was, as always, a time of great joy and celebration. The Governor of our State of Illinois was the guest speaker. The Attorney General was our Honorary Chairman. After their speeches, the first of the four alumni gave a testimonial. Roger was our last speaker. As always, he was eloquent, and then, he seemed to choke up as he spoke of his friend Ernie and how he wished he were there to share the moment. He closed and I headed toward the podium to congratulate him on the fine presentation he had made.

Then, out of the corner of my eye, I saw someone coming out of the back of the banquet hall, a young man dressed up in a brand new suit. As he came closer, I recognized it was Ernie. I stopped as he came closer to the stage. Roger went down the steps to meet him. Coming closer to the podium, they embraced, giving each other a powerful hug. Roger pointed to the mike and pleaded with Ernie to say something. Ernie was afraid and all choked up, but after the encouragement from a lot of us, he went to the microphone.

"My name is Ernie," he said. "And I'm an alcoholic." "Hi, Ernie," the audience responded. "I don't know a whole lot about life," he continued. "But one thing I know for sure. If you want to make it in this life, 'You Have to Have Love'."

Love is not getting, but giving.

—*Henry Van Dyke*

PHOTO BY JEFFREY LANGLOIS

YOU DON'T HAVE A TAPE?

"**WHAT DO YOU MEAN? YOU DON'T HAVE A TAPE!**" I asked rather indignantly.

In retrospect I guess I should have been more understanding, but here I had just been at a great, fantastic, awesome concert and they had no recording whatever of this incredible event.

"You can see when amateurs are involved," I grumbled to my wife. "Had I been part of the presentation, we would have made some real money on this event. That's why the cultural creative world needs administrators who are sales oriented." I kept mumbling, just not letting it go. They didn't even have a tape of previous concerts or anything this great community orchestra had done.

Then I heard my wife softly humming the show tunes that had been played. Oh, she couldn't hit all the notes from *Phantom* or *A Chorus Line*, and a few lines were probably missing from *Le Miz* or *West Side Story*. I started to hum with her on Evita and surely I was almost in a marching step as we were heading towards the car with the *Stars and Stripes Forever*. What a beautiful night it was—and seats were empty, I thought. The conflict was still there.

We got into the car and I turned on the radio—news, sports, something, and always something. The announcers were talking or some commercial was on, but always something in conflict with the serenity and beauty of the past moments. I turned the radio off. The beautiful, warm spring breeze was wonderful. Humming gently touched the silence of the evening. My wife's humming. In fact, we were both humming.

How could I have missed it? That wonderful evening in the middle school gym, with tunes played by a beautiful and professional community orchestra. All those wonderful tunes at a ticket price of twenty bucks apiece. No value could be put on this evening. It was like a moment on the beach looking at the sunset. You take a picture, and when it is developed, the sunset just doesn't look right. You can't feel the sand between your toes and the rhythmic sound of the surf. So many great moments in our lives happen when we least expect them. These are moments we will never have on audio equipment or film, and how beautiful those memories are.

The conversation usually starts, "Do you remember the time...?" You, it, or we believe it—a statement of fact with no confirmation of sight or sound. It will be a memory played in your mind and reaffirmed by numerous repetitions of how beautiful that moment was.

How many times have we tried to capture those special moments on tape or film only to realize that some moments were meant to be in our memories only and captured there by who and what we are. How do I miss these obvious things? Memories of our loved ones, our friends, those who bring the tears of joy to our being, and those really important things that make life really count.

We are challenged and distracted by so many things. The days are filled by so many things that distract us from that which is really important. We struggle to place significance on things that we think will in turn make us important. We say "Had they only done it my way," not sitting back and appreciating their way, no matter how inadequate we think their way is. Maybe that moment was not to be placed on tape or film. Maybe that moment was not yours to determine, but really just to appreciate. How could it be that simple and the beauty so easily missed?

"You should carry a tape recorder around with you" they said. "Then when you get an idea, you'll be able to record it." "Right" I chuckled. "Most of my singing and thinking is done in the shower. Now nothing is so profound that my water bill is increased nor is there a music contract pending anywhere. Most of the time I'll just go to bed. No one is standing there expounding in a questioning mode."

"Oh, you don't have a tape?"

So live that your memories will be a part of your happiness.

—Author Unknown

PHOTO BY JEFFREY LANGLOIS

THOSE DREADED SAND TRAPS

I SUPPOSE MY FIRST EXPERIENCE WITH FEAR OCCURRED when my father died. I was just three years old. The fear of not having that special person in my life has had a lasting impact. The fear of abandonment followed when they sent me off to military school. There were many fears when I joined the Army and was sent overseas. Each of these fears, in their own particular way, would mold my faith and test my perseverance.

After I got married, I constantly feared whether or not I had the ability to have a relationship, support a family, and live my life. Then there was alcohol. A healthy fear (along with a great deal of pain) made me change. Bypass surgery was a definite fear. It reaffirmed the reality of life, bringing it sharply into focus. My brother's death at age 44 confirmed that a healthy fear of death and subsequent preventative action is a great motivational force for change.

You would think that after all this, the fear of sand traps on a golf course would be quite insignificant. Well, now at my age, one thing that really psyches me out *are those dreaded sand traps*. I read up on how to hit out of sand: wet sand, dry sand, soft sand, heavy sand, long shots and short shots, high shots and low shots. Then there are all the different clubs and various ways to grip them, how to stand and how to swing. How can something that is supposed to be so much fun be so much work? Then there is the dress code. You can buy a good golf shirt for $70.00. You know how many dozens of fishing bait worms that is? In fact, golf has a lot of codes. Where to walk and when not to talk. More stuff to read and see than you could ever dream of.

Some of the rules challenge common sense. For instance, once I was given a sleeve of these expensive golf balls. Having been schooled as a fisherman in the past, my shots tend to go directly towards the water. As a result, I hit one of those balls right in the middle of the pond. I was so saddened when I had just lost that wonderful expensive ball that I apologized to my friend who had given it to me. Then I was informed that it would cost me a penalty stroke on top of it! I just can't understand why I love the game so much!

It was Mark Twain who said, "Golf is a good walk spoiled." Well, I think sand is a way to spoil a good day. Have you ever had something in your life that is in such total command of your mental powers—maybe even your life?

When I play golf and watch the ball heading for the sand, I visualize all the things I have dreaded in my life. They flash before me. Even non-golfers understand the pain as I try to explain my anguish and disgust with sand. But I am determined not to allow the fear of sand to gain control of my life.

My ball was in the sand again, but this time I was armed with knowledge and my convictions. Putting my head down, firmly planting my feet in the sand—you know, moving them back and forth, forcing them to dig in, I mentally reaffirmed my attitude that this would be my finest moment.

Club face open, I did not look twice at how high the sand trap edge was above me. "Impossible shot" I would have thought just a week before. A full smashing swing projected the ball over the edge and onto the side of the green. The ball slowly moved toward the hole—closer and closer. My heart started to beat faster and faster as every slow-motion rotation of the ball brought it nearer and nearer to the hole. The ball rimmed the cup and then fell in. It was one of my finest golfing moments. Johnny, who had earlier done the heckling, led the applause. "Bet you wish you had that on video!" he shouted with joy. I had accomplished what

I thought I could not do—I had conquered that dreaded sand trap.

I reflected back, on one of my friend's sayings. "You know this golf game is a lot like living. We do not own anything—we're just here renting space."

That was a fine and dandy saying, but I was not going to let some old sage's wisdom alter my excitement, even though what he said was true.

We all have dreaded sand traps. My wife has a healthy fear of water; other people fear flying. Our dreaded sand traps are real, and when we conquer that place or thing, even for just a moment, it is a moment of incredible joy. We just can't stop trying.

Now I can walk onto any golf course. My shoulders are back and my head is high. It won't make any difference any more if my next sand shot is good or bad, up and out, or down and in. One thing I do know, just like *you* know when you have overcome some obstacle...

We can beat those dreaded sand traps, whatever they are.

The week following the "impossible shot," I was in the sand trap again. This time I approached the shot with more self-assurance and I felt pride of accomplishment from my past success. However, I hit the ball right up and into the side of the trap and under a lip, putting it in a worse place than it was before I hit it. The shot was a complete failure. This time I didn't mind failure, because I know as long as I keep trying, I can hit another great shot. I guess there is only one true failure—**not trying**! That's just something I'm not going to do.

Hard things are put in our way,

not to stop us,

but to call out our courage and strength.

—Author Unknown

PHOTO BY JEFFREY LANGLOIS

HUMILITY

How many times have you looked back at something said or done and asked yourself or your higher power, "Now what was that all about?"

I am often reminded of a story about a man walking in the desert during a huge famine. As he saw millions of people dying of starvation, he looked to the heavens and asked God how he could let this tragedy happen.

God responded by saying, "I tried not to have this happen—this is not my wish."

"But you are God," the man answered, "and you can make anything happen or not happen."

"I tried to stop this," God replied. "I tried to tell mankind."

The man was desperate for a better answer and persisted with his questioning. "Well, if you tried to warn us this would occur, then why did it happen? And God answered, "Because no one listened."

How often do I ask myself during the course of a day, "Am I listening?"

Most of the time I don't know what God's will *is*, but I surely know what it *isn't*.

As a person brought up by ego-driven motivation, it was not hard for me to recognize over time that this was not the way to get though life in harmony with my fellow man. And so one day, after years of trying to work an honest program, I asked my higher power for some humility.

It was devastating. It seemed like someone had pulled the switch on all my motors. All the ego-driven forces of energy were halted. I did not know how to function as a

HUMILITY

humble person. After 72 hours I quickly asked for a reversal, hoping really for some sense of balance. Looking back, I feared that my higher power would give me little object lessons to sort of put my ego in check. That's why in my daily reflections I'll often ask, "Was there a message there for me?"

I am by nature a night person. I've never believed in the saying, "The early bird gets the worm." There are big fat birds on my feeders all day long. Watching late night television on Friday nights and sleeping in until 11:00 a.m. on Saturday morning is one of my greatest joys. So when the phone on my nightstand went off at 7:30 a.m., I was far from awake. Begrudgingly picking it up, I did not even say "good morning." It was more like "Hello, can I help you?"— an office response.

"Henry, this is Jerry," said the caller. "How are you?" Jerry was a fellow from the local Twelve Step group. Jerry had a lot to do with the business of running the local, state, and county-wide activities of the various Twelve Step groups and really did a great job making those National Conferences work. And, he was a wonderful man on top of it all.

"How are you?" he asked again, as if my response sounded like I was half dead.

"All right," I answered, "and what can I do for you?"

"I'm in a real jam, Henry," he replied. "The Annual Conference is in Chicago this weekend and our main banquet is tonight. We expect four to five thousand people."

"Yes, go on," I said.

"We are in a real jam!" he repeated. "You see our keynote speaker from California got sick and cancelled."

Now, I was waking up. In fact, I was sitting up. After all these years, the call had finally come. It wasn't unexpected; after all, I was now making about thirty motivational speeches a year for organizations like the United Way, Rotary Club, speakers bureaus, even testifying at a congressional hearing. But as a speaker, I had never been elevated beyond my local Twelve Step groups, and I just kind of accepted that as God's will.

Now, I thought, my time had finally come. This would be the beginning of my first national speaking tour. I was really awake now.

"What can I do for you," I asked enthusiastically. "Well," Jerry answered, "I know this is very short notice, but I had an emergency meeting with the events committee—and they asked me to call you.

"Yes," I answered with such enthusiasm that I was standing ready to go.

"We would like to know," Jerry continued, "do you know of anyone who might speak tonight"?

My heart fell to the floor. "Me! Me! Me!" my ego wanted to scream out, but years on the program put me in check. I was devastated and speechless. I don't even remember the conversation that followed with Jerry. I do remember I tried to help him find a speaker.

I've lived with the philosophy that attitude can change adversities into assets. I just wish my higher power wasn't so tough on me. But I guess I really needed a good dose of... **humility**.

Humility is the solid foundation

of all of the virtues.

—Confucius

PHOTO BY JEFFREY LANGLOIS

SAYING "HELLO"—SAYING "GOODBYE"

IN MY YOUTH, I NEVER WORRIED OR REALLY CONCERNED myself much with saying "Goodbye." As a matter of fact, saying "Hello" didn't mean much either.

When my father died and I was only three, it seems like all attachments to anything are embraced with thoughts of betrayal. A major part of a young life is gone with the impossibility of having any proper closure. When the remaining adults blame your mother for his death, what was I to do?

Today, when a tragedy occurs, grief therapy abounds coming from everyone and everywhere. A different lesson had to be learned in the days of my youth. You had to toughen up and struggle through it in the most inadequate ways. No tears, no remorse. You became a hardened survivor, never allowing anyone to see how vulnerable and human you really were.

I never really challenged the thought of what I had done to deserve my childhood. I learned to never express my feelings. Those things were stuffed inside. Scar tissue sealed my fate. We all know what happens when we start picking on scars—we bleed. I had been wounded deeply, even though pain was something I was not allowed to feel.

Taking me, a 12-year-old maladjusted child and putting me into a military academy surely had many serious negative consequences. Yet, the disciplines and structure probably saved my life. Just what kind of "life" is really the question?

Military minds are not developed to explore moral thoughts of man nor of serving man as stewards of love and compassion. Soldiers are trained to do bodily harm and kill if necessary. To do that you must learn to respond to commands and stuff all feelings, ignoring what the results or outcome might be. My personality, in fact every part of my being, filled that mold perfectly.

Yet, something inside of me was in conflict with that type of thinking. I trusted no one. Conflict and confrontation was a learned survival skill.

It is possible I used the biblical statement "Test everything. That which is to survive, will". It was certain alcohol entered my life as the magic elixir to numb pain and alter thoughts.

Soldiers don't verbalize when they say "Hello". They salute. This act was created to show one was not carrying a weapon of harm. They also salute when they say "Goodbye" and call each other "Sir". I learned to never say, "be seeing you," and in most cases I never would.

How then could I, so insensitive and defensive, ever have a relationship with anyone or anything? My life centered around alcohol. It truly allowed everything and nothing to happen. It became the "Alpha and the Omega", creating a false scenario to every situation and event.

Incredibly, within all that insanity, Diane and I were married. This event, in itself, challenged all consideration of reality. I had no conception of what made a relationship. I was very mixed up and full of misconceptions.

I was thirty years old with two sons, when a serious and final conflict arrived. I was faced with adversity. My alcoholism, my addiction, and denial were at a peak. I had a strong spiritual awakening. It forced me into a strong dose of righteousness and honesty. I called for help.

I didn't know why then, at the young age of 30, I had the urgency to change my life. In those days, the average addict did not work on their problem until around age 50. But, thank God, I have not had a drink, a smoke, or another serious addiction again. I am always mindful that a gift is given, "one day at a time."

I don't really know when the philosophy of the Twelve Steps started to change my life. It probably began right at the beginning when I admitted I was powerless over alcohol. It took some time to admit I was powerless over many other addictions—had I realized how sick I really was, I probably would have given up a long time ago. Many things in my life give testimony to statements and clichés of the Twelve Steps. One such philosophy is, "God won't give you more than you can handle in one day." To some, this may seem impossible!

So, as the days passed into months and years I learned to trust, to believe, to love. Love has no expectations. I learned to live with that thought. I could be disappointed by persons like me who abuse humans.

No longer would I set upon others my level of standards. I quickly came to know that the only inventory I have the right to take is mine.

When people now ask me to evaluate him or her, this or that, I respond by saying how I must take my inventory first. Each and every morning, I work on me. Usually during my conscious awareness of that task, I'm busy through the entire day. I need to stay focused on what I must do in order to be a loving friend, spouse, father and member of society. I am not preaching, but rather expressing the task my higher power has for me, in molding the day and trying to make me a man.

It is here that my compulsive, addictive behavior changed from self-will run riot to having genuine concern for other people. Before this change I had no idea what was involved in a relationship. With the tools practiced in the program, I learned to care and to express my feelings.

It's taken time and effort on my part but now I am able to listen to those I love. I now want to hear what you have to say, to appreciate your time and your love in a true spiritual way. I want to share our moments so that they can be remembered. How can I be more attentive? What would make you happy? What can we do together? It is then that those moments grow into days, months and years.

In time Diane and I would walk on the beach or the golf course. I could share a sunset or watch an impossible chip shot out of the sand into the hole. I could appreciate the excitement of the moment while catching fish with a friend. Now, life is doing things that I don't have to do—like making the bed or cleaning up after dinner or some other chore. Life is good and loving—quiet in its moments, time for peace—so that I am full of anticipation when I give a hug and say "Hello," and feel sadness when saying "Goodbye."

You will find as you look back upon your life that the moments you have truly lived are the moments when you have done things in the spirit of love.

—Henry Drummond

PHOTO BY JEFFREY LANGLOIS

ATTITUDE CAN CHANGE ADVERSITIES INTO ASSETS

It did not take me long after I entered the program to realize that there was a lot more than just the Twelve Steps. "How it Works" seems to repeat itself over and over again in my head. Rigorous honesty was stated three times. This was the key to living the program, and yet I knew it was impossible for me to do. I did not like what alcohol had done to me. I did not like what I had done to myself. To be completely honest with this monster would be too much to live with, and so I lived a long time with my character defects.

Some things seemed quite apparent. If one tried to be grateful and maintain an "Attitude of Gratitude," most things in life seemed to fall into place. The concept or philosophy,

"Do anything you desire—just don't drink" was not working among the members. Too many were getting drunk. I tried the "Attitude of Gratitude" idea for a while, but there were a lot of things that were happening to my family and friends that I was just not grateful for.

Then I learned the phrase, "There but for the grace of God go I." At one very memorable time I was involved in a head-on car accident. The fellow in the car that hit me was killed. "Just wasn't your time," they would say. This translated to me that I had no control over my destiny and that's just not true. "There but for the grace of God go I," seemed to mean the other fellow was not in God's grace. Who are we to determine when someone is or is not in God's grace? For years, I struggled trying to find the answer. Then, one night on a highway in Wisconsin, the puzzle began to unfold.

It was dark, around 7 p.m., on a cool fall evening. My son was driving. We were traveling around 55 miles per hour towing a beautiful bass boat with a large 115 horsepower engine on the back. It was a great boat. We were talking about getting a bigger one so that we could start to go fishing for salmon on Lake Michigan. I recalled we had just enough money to purchase a new station wagon for our printing company. We only had a few dollars to spare. We had looked at a car just before we left to go fishing. The salesman said that he would throw in two round trip tickets to any place in the U.S. if we bought the car before Monday. It was Sunday night.

Then it happened! The concrete highway in front of us disappeared. We later found out that the lane we were in was under construction and someone had taken away the barricades as a prank. Several hundred feet away the highway would go down an embankment to another highway below. I commanded for my son to step on the gas and turn the wheel hard left. My military voice and sense of urgency gave no place or time to question. My son did exactly as I had commanded. The action made the car and boat act like a bow whip. The boat trailer spun around, blowing the trailer wheels off. This caused an enormous amount of noise and sparks that you could see for a mile. Traffic slowed around us. We were now facing the traffic, but we were off the main road. We unloaded everything, and all was well, as we only had a few scratches. I looked up into the skies which were as clear as could be and asked the good Lord, "Just what is the asset supposed to be coming from this adversity?" I did know that everything happens in my life for a reason. I just couldn't figure out what it was this time.

To make a very long story short, we drove home that night leaving what was left of the boat, motor, and trailer in a storage lot, got a little sleep and purchased a new car with the airline tickets the following day. The car was several thousands of dollars less than expected. That savings, plus what we salvaged out of the boat and motor from the accident, was enough to pay for just the boat I wanted. It sold for half price due to a fellow going bankrupt. And to top it off, it was fully rigged for salmon fishing—complete with fishing tackle and all.

It was here that I met some wonderful fishing buddies. One had a place in Hawaii. "Why don't you take the tickets, fly to the West Coast and stay at my place. I'll charge you 50 bucks for the week," he said. The offer was too good to be true. I had not been feeling too good lately and I hesitated. A fellow I knew had gotten a heart attack while flying to Hawaii. He never made it, therefore I thought maybe I should get a physical examination before I went. My doctor said I was overreacting. I had just had an examination, and for a man 48 years old, I was fit as a racing horse. Nevertheless, I was insistent. I wanted a full exam with a treadmill

ATTITUDE CAN CHANGE ADVERSITIES INTO ASSETS

heart check. They were reluctant, but went ahead, scheduling my EKG and treadmill at night. It seemed like a time when a less than professional team would be conducting the exam. The doctor even left the room for a short time during the test.

Then something happened. There was a gap on the test sheet. They shut things down and transported me to the hospital. Under emergency conditions they performed an angiogram and placed me in a private room. My family was on the way. The doctor came into my room. "You're going to die," he said, as I was looking out the window at a very serene and peaceful view. "Well, that is, we are all going to die. But if you do not have bypass surgery immediately, your chances are 70% you will have a fatal attack within two weeks. Therefore, I've scheduled you for surgery for 8 a.m. tomorrow morning." He then turned and walked out of the room.

I stood there in shock and pain. If there's one thing the program taught me it was that I no longer had to be abused. How dare he treat me that way? Just who did he think he was, God? That, I knew, he wasn't. I went after him down the hall and grabbed his smock. It helped that he was smaller, and I pulled him back into my room.

"How dare you do that to me!" I commanded an answer, "How dare you?" He sat down on the bed and put his head down into his hands. He started to cry and got all choked up. Then he started to tell me his life's story and about being over-worked and losing his marriage by working seven days a week. This was crazy—here I was, in need of heart surgery, and I'm giving counsel to a doctor who had just told me I was going to die.

I got out of that hospital the next day. Several weeks later I had surgery at another hospital performed by one of the finest heart surgeons in the country. We were fishing together some time later and we talked about how we found out that I needed heart surgery. Had it not been for that particular chain of events—the car accident, getting the airline tickets, being invited to take a trip, and adopting the attitude that asked, "What are the assets to come from these adversities?"—I might not be here today. Now I always ask the question, for truly,

Attitude can change adversities into assets!

*Change your thoughts

and you change your world.*

—Norman Vincent Peale

PHOTO BY JEFFREY LANGLOIS

"THANK YOU, MR. HENRY"

As a child, my role models were war heroes. The press and everyone else made them bigger than life itself. They were men of inner strength who won insurmountable battles. While war heroes were getting all the press, my mother was raising four children on her own. I always felt she was falsely accused of being the cause of my father's death and was treated horribly by my grandfather. As a result, I learned how to be a champion by defending the underdog. I would defend her, as fellow soldiers would fight to the death to defend each other—fighting, dying for what was right, as they shared their last cigarette.

After high school graduation, I headed south to be with my mother who now lived in Ft. Worth, Texas. In a moment of despair I joined the army. While in the army I obtained an old 4-door Mercury that was a real joy. How I obtained it is another story. I am not proud of what I did to get it, but that car afforded me and some of the Army guys real joy. We loaded up after duty and headed for the El Paso café, a hard-core beer drinking drive-in on the hillside overlooking the Rio Grande. If you were a regular visitor and spent lots of bucks they would dedicate a song to you; mine was "Dance with me Henry." Every time they would see me coming they would flash the parking lot lights and play the song on the loudspeakers. It was quite a trip, and they got a lot of business. I loved every bit of it, because I was finally getting some recognition in life. Twice a week, and surely on weekends, I would load up the car with fellow G.I.s and show off all that attention. Truly, I was in my glory with all my buddies.

All my buddies except Billy, that is. Billy was in my squad, a wonderful man—but Billy was black. Prejudice was everywhere, and blacks did not associate in any way with whites. Billy was about my same size and came to me with a personal dilemma. He had to go to his sister's wedding and could not wear his uniform for some reason he would not disclose. I'd bet it had to do with telling them he was a sergeant and his uniform would certainly show them he wasn't. Whatever the case, he asked if he could borrow my blue suit, and I said, "Yes."

A couple of weeks later I drove my buddies to the drive-in as usual, except this time it was very different. There was no music. They turned off the lights. Over the loudspeaker a voice announced that *I* was no longer welcome. "Drink with your nigger friend from now on," it blurred out. "You don't drink here any more." The lights and sound remained off until I left. The fellows I brought got out of the car and entered the drive-in. I drove away, and went home alone.

It seemed as though my life would have many occasions where prejudices of many kinds tested me and prepared me for starting Serenity House. It was not uncommon for me to know people like Angel in my everyday work and social life.

"THANK YOU, MR. HENRY"

Angel was truly different in a wonderful sort of way. When I first met Angel she was 41 and came from Cabrini Green, a housing project in Chicago, Ill. She was a serious drug and alcohol abuser by the age of 26. During the next ten years, she lost everything—her apartment, car, job, family, friends, and all her self-esteem. She entered treatment through the judicial system and eventually came to Serenity House while on probation. The structure here was highly regimented and very difficult for her, but that was exactly what she needed at that time. She had it in her gut and was determined not to go back to what she was. She was going to make it, whatever it took. She also had that marvelous little quirk when addressing me by calling me "Mr. Henry." It was a practice she learned as a child, something little black children in the South were taught when addressing people. No matter how many times I told her she did not have to call me Mister Henry, she would say, "O.K. Mr. Henry." In that way she again was quite unique. It was not difficult to enjoy and appreciate the beautiful person she was and is today.

Angel stayed in treatment for quite some time, always graduating from one level of care to another one less restrictive, learning how to live with more and more freedom. She became a senior house resident in the Women's Independent Living Program, a position holding a great deal of respect among the other residents and staff. The independent living program was housed in a beautiful house in a very upscale neighborhood. It was in a very high-income community, which after a time, accepted the women in a most kind and genteel way. But Angel's life and program were about to be tested again.

It was on a Sunday morning. Angel and some of her friends were on their way to a Twelve Step meeting, which was their custom for quite some time. The friend who was driving had a little fender-bender and the police were called. They made them drive the car off the main road and then made them all give their identification. In making a check they said there were outstanding warrants for Angel's arrest. She protested, saying it was not true, that there was some mistake, but they would not listen. They handcuffed her and placed her in the back of the squad car. "I've lived in a treatment center for two and a half years and I am there now," she said. "You can check—I've done all my parole and have been clean and sober. Here are telephone numbers you can check." The police would have none of it and took her off to the local jail. "I am innocent!" she protested, and in parting directed her friends to call for help.

It was Sunday and the staff was not readily available to assist, but soon the beepers started buzzing. Soon her counselors and friends started to call the police station offering help and support.

It wasn't until Sunday night that we found she'd been moved to the county jail. It seemed like without any notice she was transferred to a county jail, waiting to be transferred to another county jail five times the size of the one she was in now. The fear was overwhelming and she started acting out, constantly protesting her innocence. They threatened to put her in restraints and the anxiety and fear became greater. She had done the right thing. She was not going to be sent to the jail she had been in before. The memories were almost too great to bear. It would cost $2,000 to bond her out and no one had the money. One of the guards kept trying to calm Angel down. "You have a lot of friends calling to help," she said, and then the miracles started to happen. The guard knew the Twelve Steps. "Let your higher power work," she continued. "He will answer your prayers." Angel calmed down and started to pray.

It was then that staff came to me and told me the story. All they could raise was a couple hundred dollars; could I find a way to raise the $2,000?

Serenity House does not give bond money, regardless of the situation. Angel had half of it in the bank, and the other half her family would raise, they responded, but not in time. The other county sheriffs were on the way out and we had about an hour. Would I help? If she was transferred into that other jail it would cost even more for an attorney, and chances were we would never get her out, they concluded.

There was only one way; I would have to use my own private funds. Too many alcoholics had burned me too often. It would be against everything I believed and professed. And yet,

"THANK YOU, MR. HENRY"

Angel was different in so many ways. I called my wife and told her the whole story and that time was running out. "Are you prepared to lose it all?" she asked. "And if you are, I'll stand behind you. Just hope those transport people stop for a doughnut." Diane had heard Angel's testimony at the Serenity House Annual Banquet and met her at one of the site visits. She knew there was a very, very worthy person here. But there are a lot of wonderful persons, I thought, and now would this open the floodgates for all the rest to ask for my financial help? There are no secrets when it comes to something like this. Time was of the essence now. I could not wait another minute to respond.

"O.K. I'll do it," I told the staff. "You get to the jail and stall the process. Get everyone you can to the jail. Let them know I am coming with the cashier's check. We will bond her out." Getting that check was a nightmare but I got to the jail just a few minutes before Angel was to be released to the other transports. She was standing on the other side of the glass doors, and then they were opened and she came out crying, almost falling into her counselor's arms. Tears were flowing everywhere. She even had me all choked up. Then she turned to me and wiped her eyes. "Thank you Mr. Henry," she said, and gave me a big hug. "I'll pay you back, I promise, I'll pay you back," she answered.

Within the next week I was fully reimbursed, but it would take Angel almost two years to straighten out the mess. A simple document snafu that cost the taxpayers a lot of money to clean up. Life was very difficult for Angel, but she never gave up. She struggled through it all like a beautiful butterfly that comes out of the cocoon to freedom. She got a car and insurance. She held her job through all the insanity and has kept it with promotions for over four years. Her apartment is beautiful and her family comes to visit. It is a book that could be written all on its own.

A few weeks ago Diane and I invited Angel out to Bakers Square for supper. She shared her story, which gave testimony to the fact that what she learned at Serenity House really works if you work it.

We parted with hugs and the sharing of some very sensitive moments. There was a slight drizzle and she got into

194

her car waving good by; and then she stopped and started to back up, stopped and rolled down the window. "Oh, by the way," she said "Thank you Mr. Henry."

Press On

Nothing in the world can take the place of persistence. Talent will not; nothing is more common than unsuccessful men with talent. Genius will not; unrewarded genius is almost a proverb. Education alone will not; the world is full of educated derelicts. Persistence and determination alone are omnipotent.

—Calvin Coolidge

PHOTO BY JEFFREY LANGLOIS

MOST RICHLY BLESSED

It was a beautiful Thursday afternoon during the spring of 2002. Why people would go to an annual awards banquet I could not understand, but there they were—hundreds of them—sharing the moment with each other. I was there, too, to receive an award for the "Humanitarian of the Year."

The program director announced the award and then read Webster's definition of humanitarian. "*One devoted to the promotion of human welfare and the advancement of social reforms.*" This was followed by some more accolades and words of praise. Then she announced my name, and the audience rose with resounding applause.

I was stunned and quite taken aback; truly caught off guard. In the past, when people stood as I entered a place, it was usually so they could avoid me and leave the area. This incredible reception was more than I could ever have imagined. The definition of humanitarian kept bouncing around in my head. As I tried to decipher it, a strange phenomenon occurred. I was standing at the podium with the award in my hand and the applause continued. I looked out into the audience, knowing inside that they were not really applauding me—for I did not truly think I was the person they were awarding. They finally quieted down and took their seats. I needed a moment of silence to collect my thoughts and get some composure.

"I did not do these things for you," I announced. There was a deadly silence, some uneasy motions, and a sort of gasp or two.

"I did these things for me," I continued. "Before *you*, I thought of my life as having little or no value. Having had by-pass surgery, which resulted in a major identity crisis, I felt I could do nothing. It seemed like my life had become a wasteful use of the Twelve Steps. Just how many times can you hear the same stories over and over again? I had burned out with little hope of having a life with purpose. I seemed to have placed myself into a nonexistent life—no place to turn and not caring if I lived at all."

Now I really had everyone's attention. "It was hearing your quiet voice calling me to serve my fellow alcoholics and drug addicts that started to change my life. It was responding in fear of losing everything that gave my life value. *You needed me, and in responding I found myself*. We came to find a common spirit, a sort of bonding in a mutual cause to save each other for a common goal. We were connected. In answering each other's call we had listened to our higher power. As we've been told, 'what we cannot do alone, we can do together.' Truly it was you who gave my life value. Each and every one of you should get this award, for you are truly the humanitarians."

Some years ago, I came upon a verse which sums up the very purpose of my life. It is known as the Prayer of the Unknown Confederate Soldier and I would like to share it with you here.

I asked God for strength, that I might achieve
I was made weak, that I might learn humbly to obey

I asked for health, that I might do greater things
I was given infirmity, that I might do better things

I asked for riches, that I might be happy
I was given poverty, that I may be wise

I asked for power, that I might have the praise of men
I was given weakness, that I might feel the need of God

I asked for all things that I may enjoy life
I was given life, that I might enjoy all things

I got nothing that I asked for
But everything that I had hoped for

Almost despite myself, my unspoken prayers were answered.
I am among all men, most richly blessed!

—Author Unknown

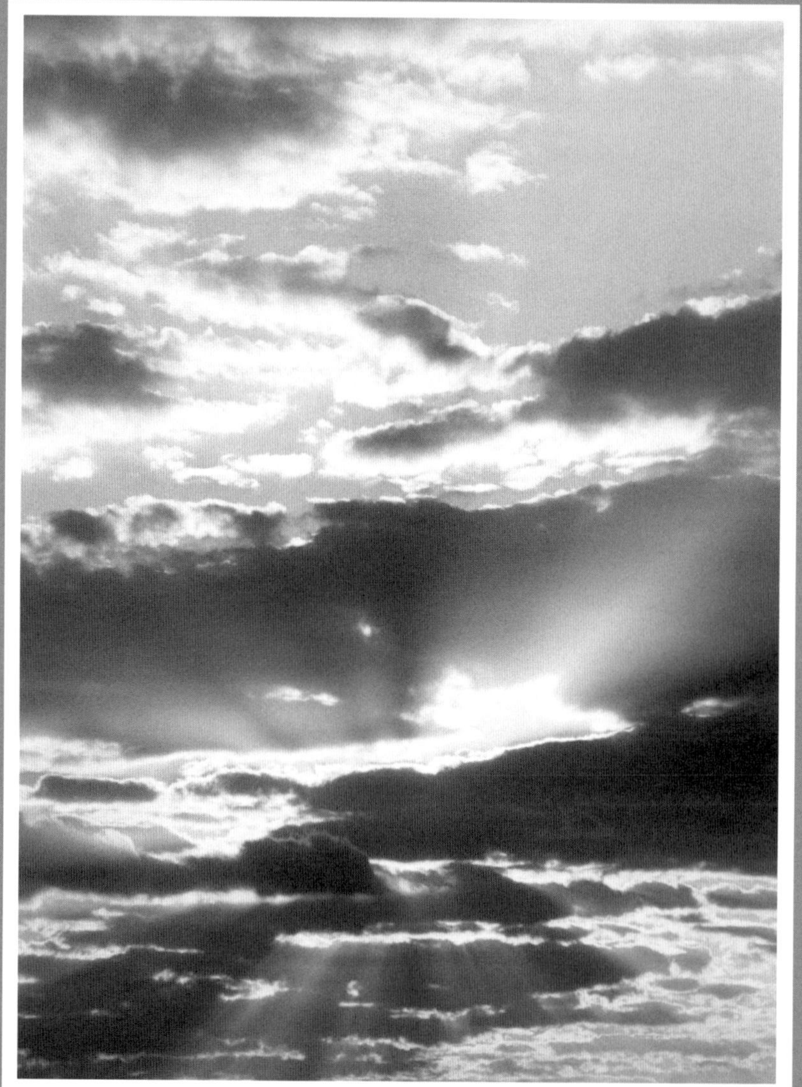

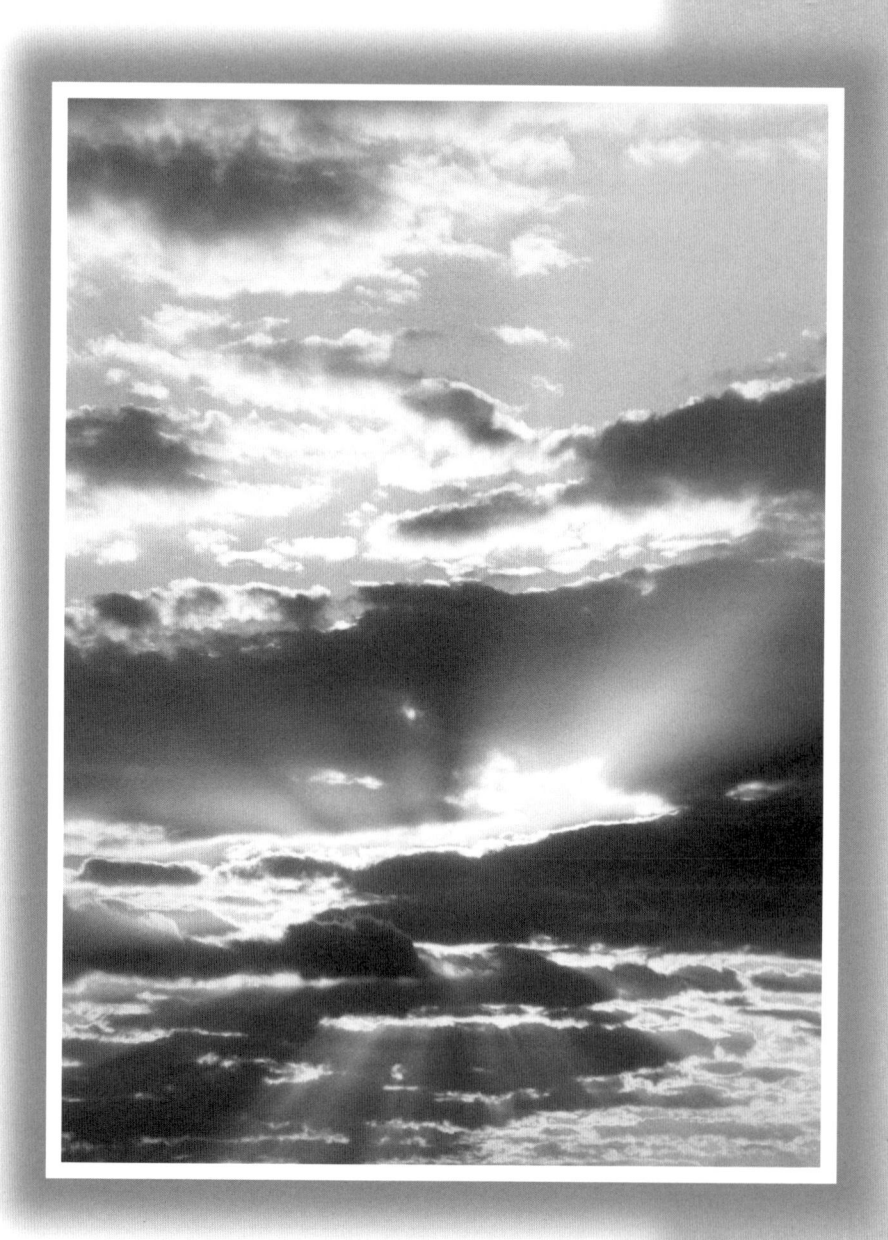

A TRILOGY OF MIRACLES

Those of us who live in the western suburbs of Chicago know all too well the hazards of highway 59 as it changes in width between north and south. At one particular location, near the Fox Valley Mall, it separates with quite a wide median strip of grass, trees, and left turn lanes.

I was traveling south in the left hand lane at the posted speed of 45 m.p.h. It was about 4:30 p.m.

Within an instant a car traveling north seemed to hit the curb on its left side and propel into mid-air coming directly at me. It seemed as if I were in a James Bond type movie. The other car was turning over—spinning like some sort of a stunt. I slammed on my brakes as the car landed on its top right in front of me.

I jumped out of my car and ran toward the upside down vehicle. Kneeling down I looked into the driver's side window. "Are you O.K.?" I asked. A young lady replied, "I'm O.K., I've got my seat belt on."

A woman behind me was screaming, "Don't touch her she might have a broken back." Fearing a possible fuel leak, I asked, "Can you release the seatbelt?" "I already have," she answered. "Can you help me out of here?" she shouted. Strangely, all the glass was gone. She came out of the car through the window without a scratch. We helped her sit on the grass and the paramedics arrived. Since she had not a scratch and sounded okay, I left her to continue on my way home. I was wondering what the message was in all of that.

I have always tried to relate events in my life to God's message for me. "There are no accidents," a spiritual friend once told me.

I suppose now is a good time to note that all the parts of this trilogy occurred during a time period of less than 2 weeks.

The second part began when I was bringing my boat to shore, planning to pick up my son and two granddaughters for their annual fishing trip with Grandpa.

"Save them!" A woman was yelling from shore, repeating it over and over, "Save them!" For a time I thought she had some religious conviction that demanded her trying to convert all of us at the state park. "Save whom?" I yelled back. "Look behind you," she answered. I did. There behind me were two very large men and a dog in the water, with an upside down canoe.

They had one small, child-sized life jacket between them. Another fisherman joined me to help. Their size was working against them, hindering their attempt to upright the canoe half full of water. It just kept turning over again and again, hitting them in the process. At times there were some pretty good blows. They were surely going to drown if they kept that up.

I yelled for them to stop and just hold onto the canoe. I would tow them in, but panic had taken over and they just kept thrashing in the water and yelling, "Save the dog!"

The other fisherman was young and seemed very strong. His boat was low to the water, a johnboat. He seemed to be outfitted to hunt as well as fish so that's probably why he agreed to go after the dog. He was really struggling to get that dog in his boat.

In the meantime, against my wishes, these two men almost swamped my boat as they tried to get in. In the process, their canoe was tied onto my boat. One of them lunged at me, almost pulling me out of my boat and into the water. One let go of the canoe and swam to the young man's boat. In the next few minutes, I told the second fisherman to just hold onto the canoe and I would tow him in. Instead he swam toward the other boat, which was filled with fishermen and gear. Remarkably, without swamping it, he got in that boat and we all went to shore.

Unscrambling the gear and uprighting the canoe went well. Despite them being wet and in some degree of shock, they were okay.

"Thanks," they said, "we'll leave the dog at home next time," as if all this was somehow the dog's fault. I still can't imagine how it all happened and no one drowned. I said, "You're welcome," and proceeded to take my son and grandchildren fishing. They made a point of warning us to wear our life jackets.

A few days later after a full day of fishing, I was driving through the countryside. I started reflecting on those two dramatic occurrences, feeling that there had been enough excitement for one week. Often, when I meditate, I ask myself what was God's plan in all of this. I came up with a blank. I started to think about the beautiful day that had just passed. I had fished with a man named Denny, a wonderful new fishing acquaintance who also is an excellent fisherman. How the good Lord places these people in my life, I'll never know, but I am surely grateful. My friend doesn't net his big fish; he just lets them roll over and then lifts them in the boat with the palm of his hand on their back—that's something to see. We had some great moments together.

The country road cut through the tall corn. It was quite dark, as there were no highway lights. The speed limit was 55 m.p.h.; the traffic was very light. Coming out of that setting toward a lit intersection seemed like a space odyssey. The signal lights facing me were green. Then, from the left,

I saw a light flash and go up into the air. I slammed on the brakes and stopped right in the center of the intersection, a premonition of what I did not know. Thank God, there was no one behind me.

Then, as if coming out of the air, a motorcycle with a huge man astride landed right in front of my car. His face was full of shock and anger. His eyes showed fear as he shouted a great many obscenities, referring to someone who must have hit him in the rear, thus forcing him up in the air in front of my car. Without a doubt, had I not stopped, I would have run over him. "I'll get him," he swore, and drove off. I proceeded through the intersection, pulled into a mini-mall nearby and just sat there. What was going on? How many more of these unexplained situations can one person experience? What was the message and why so dramatic, each being a possible life and death event. My psyche was in overload. What is the message and who were the messengers?

One message was certain. Out of all these experiences, I did not know any of the people who could have easily lost their lives, and they did not know me.

John has been a good friend of mine, and of Serenity House, for a long time. Every couple of years he'll arrange a guest appearance for me at his local philanthropic group and ask me to make an appeal for Serenity House financial assistance.

At one meeting I presented the Trilogy of Events and afterwards, a group of us shared as to how we interpreted the situations and why. The answers were as many and as different as the people in the room. The culmination of the stories was so provocative, they dared to stretch our imaginations and yet what occurred was real.

Then John's wife Jacquie said, "They are a Trilogy of Miracles!"

"How do you explain a miracle?" I asked. Someone in the group responded, "You believe!"

It was later that my good friend, Angie Zoloto, commented after hearing the stories, "It's obvious to me the good Lord is telling you that you are not done yet! These dramatic events were to make an impact on you, or sort of a wake-up call that you are really needed!"

So then I thought, *maybe miracles are not so much for those who are saved, but for those who are doing the saving.*

There are only two ways to live your life.

One is as though nothing is a miracle.

The other is as though everything is a miracle.

—*Albert Einstein*

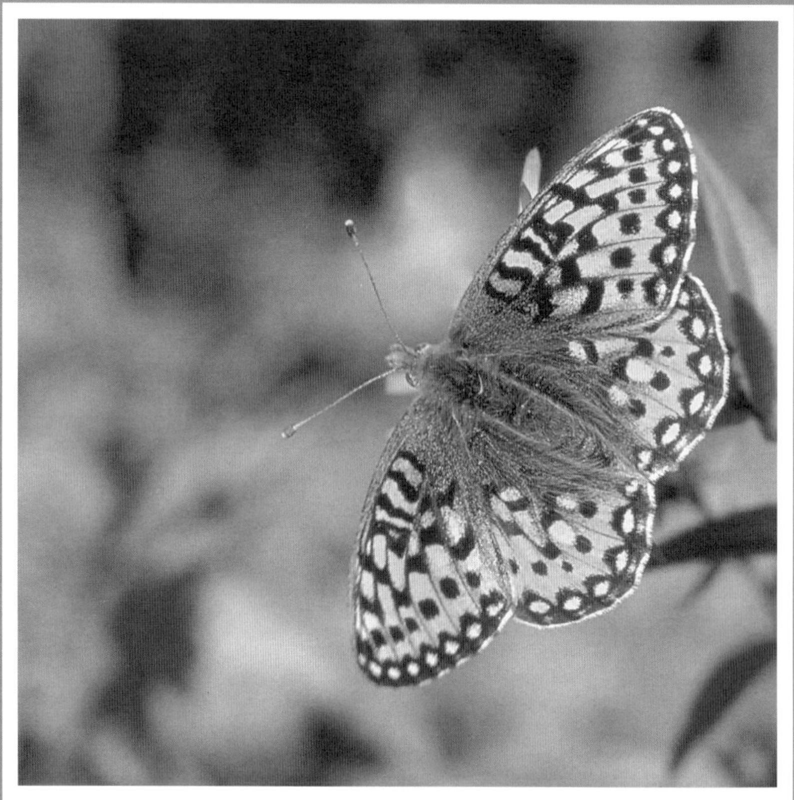

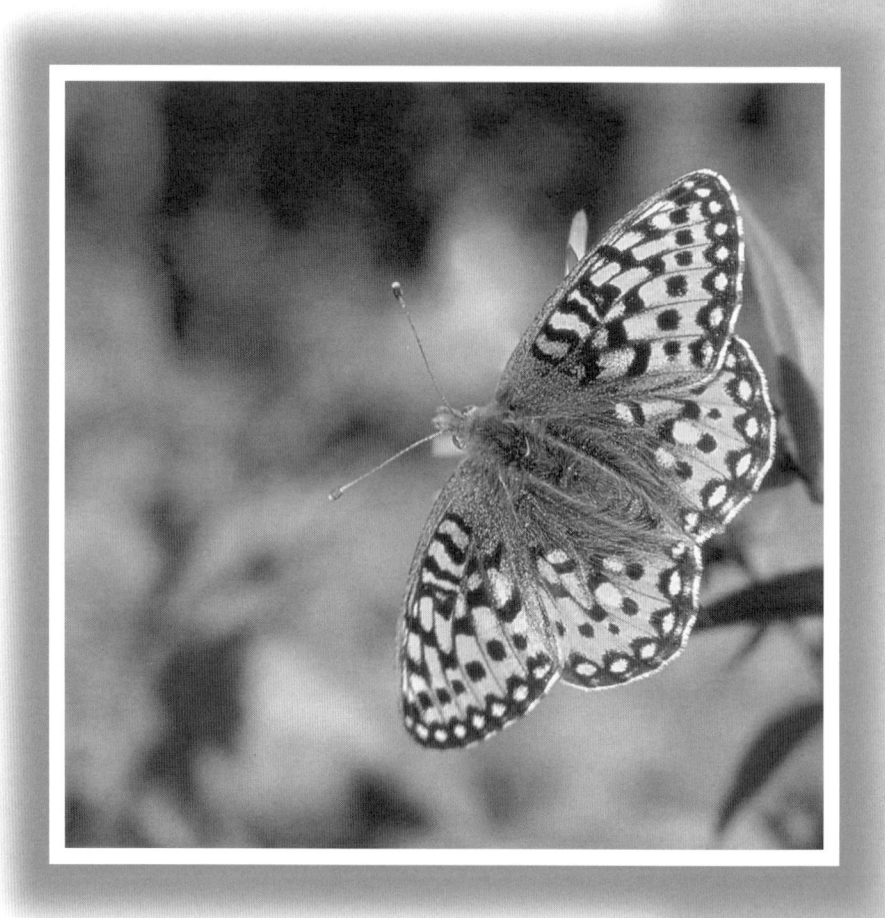

ANOTHER FAVORITE STORY TO LIVE BY: THE STRUGGLE

A MAN FOUND A COCOON OF AN EMPEROR MOTH. He took it home so that he could watch the moth come out of the cocoon.

On the day a small opening appeared, he sat and watched the moth for several hours as the moth struggled to force the body through that little hole. Then it seemed to stop making any progress. It appeared as if it had gotten as far as it could and it could go no farther. It just seemed to be stuck.

Then the man, in his kindness, decided to help the moth, so he took a pair of scissors and snipped off the remaining bit of the cocoon. The moth then emerged easily. But it had a swollen body and small, shriveled wings. The man continued to watch the moth because he expected that, at any moment, the wings would enlarge and expand to be able to support the body, which would contract in time. Neither happened! In fact, the little moth spent the rest of its life crawling around with a swollen body and shriveled wings. It never was able to fly.

What the man in his kindness and haste did not understand was that the restricting cocoon and the struggle required for the moth to get through the tiny opening was the way of forcing fluid from the body of the moth into its wings so that it would be ready for flight once it achieved its freedom from the cocoon. Freedom and flight would only come after the struggle. By depriving the moth of a struggle, he deprived the moth of health.

Sometimes we make the mistake of cutting the spiritual cocoons of others. There is a balance in helping other people. We are called to rescue the perishing (Proverbs 24:11), weep with those who weep (1 Corinthians 12:26), and help our brother in need (1 John 3:17–18). But at other times we interfere with God's work, if we intervene (e.g. 2 Thessalonians 3:6–15). There are some burdens we can't and shouldn't carry for others. If we take all the struggle away, we cut God's spiritual cocoon. Addiction groups call it "enabling."

In some cases, it is actually an unloving act to help people. When we help people who are able to help themselves, we are in fact "enabling" them to remain immature and weak.

Instead we are to "speak the truth in love" to them (Ephesians 4:15,25; Matthew 18:15; Proverbs 9:8; Luke 17:3), encourage them (1 Thessalonians 5:14), and pray for them (Ephesians 6:18). But when it is God's plan, don't be afraid to let people emerge from their cocoon to become the butterfly that God intended.

Some succeed because they are destined to,

but most succeed because they are determined to.

—Roscoe Dunjee

PHOTO BY JEFFREY LANGLOIS

THE GREATEST LESSON EVER LEARNED

MANY YEARS AGO, WHEN I WAS IN HIGH SCHOOL, I was introduced to the Greek writer and philosopher, Socrates. If my memory serves me right, he wrote a story about a group of owls sitting on a single branch. It seems they were all perched upright, hooting their normal "who," except one, who was hanging on upside down and asking "Why?"

We wake up each morning of our lives to begin a daily adventure. Many people have prearranged agendas, leading us to believe they have predestined goals and objectives. Others have some euphoric, clandestine place in space, way above normal, average thinking. As a result, these others go and do their thing. Most of us live our lives in a simple state of mind. We survive with basic truths and wisdom confused by history and primarily negative local newspapers or other media. This forces us to struggle to find our true purpose in life. It is so simple it dares not to be discovered.

When I came into the Twelve Step program, I was advised not to ask, "Why?" "Why doesn't matter," they would say. "Just pray for the willingness to accept the things you cannot change." "Why must I change?" I asked. I recall what my friend Bob in Florida said. "You either change your lifestyle or your lifestyle will change you." That was so basic, and yet it was an answer to a simple "Why?" I still struggled with the bigger picture.

I have a remarkable friend, named Henry. The two of us were recently in the same place receiving an honor. There are no accidents in God's plan. I was standing in the hallway for a mini post-award camera session when Henry came out of the County Board room with his award in hand. We graciously congratulated each other and then he said "Henry, your acceptance speeches are getting better and better and better." I was elated! My mentor was complimenting me and my ego was stimulated into looking for more. I quickly responded "Thank you. How are they getting better?" "Well," Henry said quite simply, "They keep getting shorter and shorter and shorter!"

In the early stages of starting Serenity House a similar message came from a person I consider a spiritual associate. It seemed that no one wanted to invest his or her funds or time to help an addict try to stay sober. It appeared as if my higher power was showing me that the miracle of Serenity House was truly his work in progress. I knew the Twelve Step community would never support the project. I had to become an individual that people would invest in. Even though the need for a halfway house was obvious, in the world of 'denial', they wanted to 'kill the messenger'. Many possible supporters had a great deal of influence and demanded anonymity for fear that association with me would create an unwanted stigma.

Even the government agencies created specifically to address community needs deliberately tried to sabotage my efforts. The cause needed a champion…a Man of La Mancha. This need was in direct contrast to the concept of the Twelve Steps that demanded a goal and objective toward humility. I had heard of great men and women who could do those things. I never even considered myself to be cut from that cloth.

I came to my friend Henry saying that I believe in what Dag Hammarskjold said, " Woe to the man who must live up to his testimonials". Henry replied, "Maybe it is better to say, blessed are those who try to live up to their testimonials."

As we campaigned for recognition in those early years, I became increasingly aware of my higher power working through me. I received honors and recognition. My ego was at constant war with the task of trying to stay humble. At times the task seemed unbearable, almost as though I was being torn apart.

One day while speaking with Fr. Walsh, a mentor and original board member, I expressed my feelings. "I can't go on with this. I cannot be a role model!" I seemed to yell out in pain. He looked at me and said in a positive tone of voice, "You are old enough. You should try!" Again, how could a complex struggle come to such a simple conclusion? "Why me Lord?" I would ask and a friend said, "Why not you!"

And so in conclusion, it's okay for all of us to be where we are...to live in a day preceded by history and looking into a tomorrow of hopes and visions. Still aware of our limitations, we are going to push outward against boundaries seemingly created by those who wish to intimidate us. Our wisdom has made us freer than yesterday. We no longer use guilt as a motivating force. We know where we are. What's more important is that we can humbly accept and go on. There is a lot of good in all of us that we can use to profess a greater cause of serving others. Not soup with a sermon but a loaf of bread with a lot of love.

For me, and I do mean me—one person's means to accomplish their end may not be another's. Each day I remind myself of the greatest lesson I've ever learned. It came from a childhood song. It goes like this…

Jesus loves me, this I know,

For the Bible tells me so.

Give what you have.

To someone, it may be better

than you dare to think.

—Henry Wadsworth Longfellow

Henry Tews is the Founder and CEO of Serenity House in Addison, Illinois, a non-profit, community-based treatment facility for those suffering from the disease of alcoholism and chemical dependency. He has served on the Governor's Task Force for Substance Abuse, the Special Supreme Court Committee on Lawyers Assistance Programs, and has testified before Congress regarding the Fair Housing Act of 1997. The father of five and grandfather of nine is a well-known speaker and community leader who has taught college level classes on starting a social services agency specializing in recovery. He lives in Glen Ellyn, Illinois with his wife Diane.

ABOUT THE AUTHOR

Henry's family was pleased to share their insight into the husband, father and man they love and share a life with.

HIS WIFE, DIANE WROTE...

During a recent meeting at Serenity House, Henry received written comments from the staff. They were more than heart-warming. I cannot believe that these people were talking about the same man that I have known for over forty years. Life with Henry was never dull. His mind was always restless and only recently have we seen signs of an inner tenderness. I won't question where the "old" Henry went, because those of us in his family are thrilled with the dramatic change that has come over him in recent years.

His love for his family was demonstrated in practical matters and our physical needs were always met. His military training was evident in the take charge way in which he ran his home, family and business. He defines love as unconditional—we know and trust that he will go to any length for us.

Serenity House offers Henry the opportunity to reach out to those suffering from substance abuse and he is able to see beauty in individuals that others may overlook. Memories of Henry's anger are fading and I am enjoying the new man in my life.

FROM SON CHRIS...

My dad is a passionate, determined visionary and leader. I am successful today because of the discipline he taught me as he

ABOUT THE AUTHOR

encouraged me to work outside of my comfort zone. He allowed me every opportunity to stretch the limits, fail and learn.

He always gives of himself for his family. I remember countless fishing trips where we looked for worms after a good strong rain. I recall fixing things with him around the house, hanging the pickle swing from the tallest tree. We worked together on my Pinewood Derby cars and Balsa Rockets. He sent us to private school and set a good example by attending mass with his family on Sundays.

My father finds his direction in the Serenity prayer and I am proud to say that it guides my life as well.

SON DAVID SHARED...

I always knew my father could save me from a sticky situation because he always found the perfect solution in times of crisis. I feared losing him, but when his temper flared and he was too demanding in his expectations, I sometimes wished he would go away. Life was rarely calm.

Dad has good values and goals, and when the world puts obstacles in his way, he gets angry and pushes harder. Eventually, he may see a compromise or solution, but he only gives in after a hell of a fight.

Later in life Dad started using the words "I love you." However, throughout my childhood his actions always showed me his love as protector, rescuer, provider, advisor, and disciplinarian.

FROM DAUGHTER JENNIFER...

While growing up, my biggest fear was that I might disappoint my dad. I was the only girl with four older brothers, so he was very strict, refusing to let me do everything I wanted.

I was offered an internship in the record business, which he vetoed since he did not want me in that environment. Being Henry's daughter, I had learned to negotiate and talked my parents into giving their permission, which opened the door to my career.

As I got older, I feared losing him to heart failure, and also began to see a different side of my father. He has more appreciation for the things and people in his life. I have watched my dad grow, as much as he has watched me. The moment he followed his dream to begin Serenity House, he changed.

I have taken on some of his characteristics in my work ethic, loyalty and semi-dramatic reaction to life's event. He also taught me to grab opportunities.

FROM SON JASON...

Twice I was frightened by my father's brush with death and the possibility that he would not be with me. The first was a car accident in which the other driver did not survive. I visited the accident scene and saw the blood, my father's blood, streaking down the side of his van, and where his hand went through the windshield. It was a frightful moment.

The next was when he suffered a heart attack that required bypass surgery. When the doctor told me his condition, I cried. I could not bear to think of life without my father. He would not see my future children and the kids' baseball games. He would not see the guidance and wisdom that he instilled in me come to fruition.

Dad believes in tough love. I wanted to drop out of school in my first year of college. He looked me in the eyes and asked where I was going to live and work because I was over eighteen and would not be living in his house. I realized he was right and that I should finish school. He would risk my defiance to prove to me that I was not making a wise choice.

My father was very clear about what he wanted with no room for creative interpretation, although I do not remember him being disappointed in me. My parents taught us what love is, and how love can keep you together in the hard times and keep you humble when things are going well.

AND LASTLY FROM SON HENRY...

As a parent and business owner, I can appreciate the many gifts my dad has given me. It has taken a long time for me to realize all that I have been taught.

My father taught us the value of hard work at a young age and shared its rewards. I have learned that I could make any decisions I wanted to, but that I alone would live with the results of my actions. Dad always picked me up when I fell. To this day, I know that if I needed him, he would be on his way.

My father is the purest example of the phrase; lead, follow or get out of the way. He is a great leader. He has started two successful organizations. I wonder what is next; hopefully (for the sake of his challengers) just fishing and golf.

REFLECTIVE NOTES

REFLECTIVE NOTES

REFLECTIVE NOTES